# MEET YOUR DOG

# MEET YOUR DOG

## the GAME-CHANGING GUIDE to UNDERSTANDING YOUR DOG'S BEHAVIOR

BY **KIM BROPHEY**, CDBC, CPDT-KA

FOREWORD BY RAYMOND COPPINGER

PHOTOGRAPHS BY JASON HEWITT

CHRONICLE BOOKS
SAN FRANCISCO

*Dedicated to the late Raymond Coppinger—the father of the modern canine science movement, whose life's work revolutionized our understanding of dogs.*

*Your honesty, humor, and friendship were never lost on those of us lucky enough to know you.*

Library of Congress Cataloging-in-Publication Data is available.

ISBN 978-1-4521-4899-1
Manufactured in China

Design by Hillary Caudle

10 9 8 7 6 5 4 3 2 1

Chronicle Books LLC
680 Second Street
San Francisco, CA 94107
www.chroniclebooks.com

# CONTENTS

# FOREWORD

Raymond Coppinger

*Professor Emeritus of Biology, Hampshire College*

I wish I had read this book fifty years ago when I first started to train dogs.

Back then I was a college professor with a team of sled dogs, which were part of my professional academic research. I published dozens of scientific papers, often with my students, about the neurophysiology and anatomy that help make a successful sled dog.

Toward the end of the 1970s, my wife Lorna and I started the Livestock Guarding Dog Project at Hampshire College, where we raised and trained pups to protect American sheep from predation. Eventually we had records on over 1,500 dogs, most of them descendants of the original imports that we had collected in Eurasia as breeding and working stock. We placed them on farms and ranches where they did a brilliant job defending livestock.

In those early days of introducing this relatively unknown type of sheep dog to Americans, people would ask if you could train a dog to both herd and guard sheep. Could one dog do both jobs? We didn't know the answer. So Lorna and I went to Scotland on our way home from a field trip with a pile of puppies from Italy and Yugoslavia, and bought ourselves six border collies. Many of the pups were born on the same day. Thus, we had a controlled experiment going where we raised those pups in a large pen for almost a year and watched their behavioral development. What we found was that each breed was different in the timing of their development. They also acquired very different kinds of behaviors.

So, we got our answer: No—dogs did not develop with joint guarding and herding abilities.

It was during that experiment that I acquired the most difficult dog of my life—Jane, one of the six Scottish border collies. She was an intense drover's dog, so when I put her on a mountain road behind 3,000 sheep, she would work all day long pushing them up the mountain. We herding guys would sit trouble arises in canine paradise, it's often because we as owners have lost sight of (or never knew about) certain critical factors that affect our dog.

It's far too easy to get caught up in the romantic notion of the "perfect" companion, holding every dog to a single black-and-white standard of our imagined ideal. In reality, of course, there is no such thing as a "good" or "bad" dog, any more than there is a "good" or "bad" human partner. What it comes down to is largely just compatibility between two creatures' basic natures, needs, and circumstances. Getting exasperated about all the stuff we don't like about our friend—taking it personally and trying to change him according to our fixed standard—is simply a waste of time. Though well-intentioned, our habit of treating every dog generically according to our concept of what a "good dog" is, while disregarding their inherent differences, may pave the way to some seriously undesirable ends.

For Rebecca and her dog, Dexter, the bump in the road of their love story came when she moved into her new mountain home. Two years earlier, when she decided to purchase a Wheaten Terrier puppy from a breeder, she knew she was getting a highly active and intelligent dog. She was up for the challenge, and raised her wickedly adorable little pup from the age of eight weeks old on her family farm in Tennessee. They spent their days together hanging about in barns and fields. She made sure he had the best food, health care, and provisions from day one. It was a fairy tale, and they were on track for a happily-ever-after future.

And then life happened. When Dexter was two years old, a family member of Rebecca's who was having health issues needed some support, so Rebecca and Dexter left the farm and set down new roots. They settled into a little cabin in the woods near Asheville, North Carolina. After just three weeks in the new house, Rebecca found herself at the veterinarian's office asking about the possibility of Prozac for a suddenly psycho dog, who had "gone completely bonkers, literally spending his entire day barking and scratching at my walls. What on earth is wrong with him?" She feared that the recent move had triggered some latent genetic abnormality, an obsessive-compulsive disorder that caused him to endlessly run along her walls—digging, yipping, and frothing at the mouth. She wondered about neurotic shadow-chasing behavior she had read about online; did Dexter have that condition?

Things were coming to a head very quickly, and the looming cloud over their once-perfect relationship showed no signs of clearing. Rebecca reported that Dexter hadn't eaten in forty-eight hours, and neither of them had slept in days. Dexter had no interest in going for a walk other than to relieve himself, dragging her back to the house to scamper violently along the walls once again. He wouldn't play ball. He refused her affection. The once-perfect pair was in deep trouble.

Rebecca asked her vet for a diagnosis and a prescription to help her friend. Instead, she was given my phone number. Her vet suggested she consult with a qualified dog behavior consultant before putting him on any medication, just to be sure they weren't missing anything.

As I sat on Rebecca's sofa in her lovely new cabin and observed Dexter's curious behavior, I had an instant suspicion. Though Dexter did look a little nuts while he was doing it, his behavior seemed perfectly appropriate to me—if my suspicion was correct.

"I don't think Dexter is crazy at all," I said. "I think you have mice in your walls. If I'm right, he's just working very hard to do his terrier job. And he's getting really frustrated because he can't reach the little buggers." Rebecca's face reflected her total surprise, embarrassment, and relief. I crossed my fingers that I was right as I handed her a referral to another specialist—my trusted exterminator. Dexter might simply be following his instinct as a dog designed to destroy rodents. Rebecca thought terriers were cute, with their wiry hair and long beards; she hadn't considered what a terrier actually was in the first place, how he might be different from all the other dogs she had known. Suddenly, all that time Dexter had spent running around behind the haystacks in the barn in Tennessee made a lot of sense, too.

Three days later, Rebecca called me, laughing, to say that her walls were indeed infested with mice. Traps had been set; and already Dexter's behavior was a little less intense. Her natural varmint hunter who had secretly rid her family's barns of mice for two years on the old farm had found himself in a sudden predicament when he was unable to get at the mice. Inside his new home, his genes had collided with his environment and quickly turned into an addiction that wreaked havoc on their daily lives. Thank goodness, I thought, that she had the benefit of the big picture. She didn't come to drastic conclusions about Dexter's behavior, mistreat his symptoms, or give up on her wonderful friend after an exasperating period of frustration and sleep deprivation. We got to the bottom of Dexter's behavior quickly and were able to put our efforts toward addressing the source of the problem right away. The rodents in the walls had been exciting his terrier instincts into madness.

It's not always so simple, to be sure. Relationships are complicated, and the ones we share with our dogs are no exception. Sometimes the solutions are not as handy as a phone call to pest control. But they may be. The only way you will know, and be able to get through the rough patches with your friend when they arise, is to get a clear picture of what you're dealing with.

Sometimes, the most valuable therapy is the one that helps us to see the big pink elephant in the room. Looking at our big pink elephant of a dog, and understanding and accepting him for who and what he is, can be a powerful and transformative exercise. Getting clear about the critical factors that affect our dogs is the first step to finding and maintaining healthy relationships with them as their conscientious stewards and friends. This is a necessary and powerful undertaking. We need to unravel our assumptions and expectations about these canine partners of ours. We start by examining, and challenging, a broken cultural concept—the pet dog.

## The Fairy-Tale Pet

We get a dog. We take him home and give him a name. We buy him food, a bed, some toys, a leash, a collar with his name on it. We take him to the vet to get his shots. We take him out on walks, brush his coat, and kiss him good-night. He is our "pet."

Most of us were born into a world in which the idea of a pet dog is normal, but not so many years ago, the entire idea was pretty absurd. While dogs may have been pets on a relative scale in various cultures throughout history, the practice of bringing them into our homes as captive full-time consumers and family members is far more recent. It is also mostly unique to modern developed countries like the United States. The entire pet industry has emerged—and subsequently exploded—in little more than sixty years, feeding an impractical and unrealistic perception of the dogs in our lives in order to attract our attention to their more marketable "needs."

In 2016, Americans spent over 62 billion dollars on their pets, a figure projected to keep growing by leaps and bounds. A Pet Industrial Complex has emerged to cater to the billions of dollars consumers are willing to spend—from beef-flavored Prozac to smocked dresses and spa treatments for dogs.

Endless gourmet treats and toys, day-care visits, dog-park playdates, personal groomers and trainers, and better medical and dental care than many Americans receive—these are the standard amenities for many pet dogs. Born, as most of us were, into this pet-dog era, we rarely question these preconceptions and practices.

In recent times, dog behavior problems have become increasingly common and severe, with communities struggling to navigate everything from bites and lawsuits to overcrowded shelters filled with unwanted dogs. This means that certain myths about the needs and natures of our so-called pet dogs need to be examined. Every day in my practice, I pass a box of tissues to another desperate dog lover sharing deep frustrations and heartache in their first consultation. A few examples:

🐾 *Wally cracked a tooth breaking out of the crate and destroyed the Persian rug and new designer curtains, so Donna and her husband have given up date nights and Sunday drives in order to take turns babysitting the dog 24-7 and to help cover the bills.*

🐾 *Buddy and Boomer have been fighting so much that they have to be separated at all times and can no longer be walked together. This doubles the amount of time Ron spends trudging around the neighborhood in the dead of winter waiting for the dogs to pee instead of helping the kids with their homework.*

🐾 *No one in Patty's house has had a full night's sleep since they brought Dolly back to Manhattan after that trip to the Smoky Mountains. Her howling at sirens has resulted in three noise violations in three weeks.*

🐾 *Leroy won't let Lexi's new boyfriend back in the bed at 3 a.m..; she had to remove the little snarling beast from his arm two nights ago. The guy has, understandably, dropped a few sour hints that she needs to choose between him and the dog.*

Like thousands of other unhappy dog owners, these clients had been searching diligently—if unsuccessfully—for answers to their dogs' behavior problems. Internet searches, advice from friends, and reruns of dog training shows turned up some pretty confusing information. What they were finding and hearing just didn't add up. Intuitively, they sensed something profound was missing.

This is the missing link: we don't have the big picture. We have forgotten that dogs are animals. We have forgotten that there are major differences between different types of dogs, so we fail to meet their specific behavioral needs. We struggle to train them to be as we wish them to be, expecting the wrong behaviors from our canine companions. We need to understand that it's not their behavior but *our expectations about their behavior* that are broken. Our pet culture has failed to question the fundamental soundness of what we ask of our dogs in our day-to-day lives—when we have company over, when we pass other dogs on the street, when we leave our dog alone in a crate for over ten hours a day, when the neighborhood kids barrel through the front door at all hours unannounced. There are very good reasons why some dogs handle these kinds of events with ease, and why others come apart at the seams. Put simply: We can't have the same expectations for a German Shepherd that we would for a Pug. Treating all dogs as if they were the same—operating from a standard recipe and ignoring their elemental variations—sets them (and us) up for certain failure.

On the flip side, you are about to consider the common ground shared by various dogs as you never have before. You are also going to see that you and your dog have more in common than you realized. In my experience, this discovery is a joyful one that leads to a new appreciation for your dog's life experiences, and will challenge any existing perceptions of him as a "pet."

In this book, you will be given a new way to understand your dog's behavior so that you have a shot at a love that lasts, built on true understanding.

While anthropomorphizing your dog is not the goal, this book does encourage you to consider your dog with a new kind of empathy. Though there are some big differences between you and your dog, this book operates from the basic tenet that your dog is a sentient being having an individual experience on this earth just like you. There is just as great a danger in the kind of reverse anthropomorphism that would cause us to assume a dog's experience couldn't possibly be similar to our own; in doing so, we risk dismissing the animal experience as less than ours.

If we are bold enough to extend a true compassion—one built upon a deep understanding—rather than just sympathy, towards our dogs as we try to understand their behavior, we take a necessary first step toward an authentic relationship with them. If you are reading this book, you are about to take a giant leap forward. You are about to experience an entirely different kind of bond with your dog. But first, let's clear just a little more baggage out of the way.

## Bad Eggs and Dropped Balls

When things go wrong, such as a dog bite, it's so tempting to point a finger. We often default to the age-old debate of *nature vs. nurture.*

One prevalent cultural myth is "It's all how you raise them": the notion that dogs are blank slates on which we write our own influence through *nurture* (raising, training, care, or medication). The notion that we can prevent potential behavior problems with basic obedience training or simply "rehabilitate" problem pets into "fixed" ones through such measures is simplistic and naïve. Solid training practices and healthy provisions can go a long way toward ensuring better chances at success and can exact remarkable changes in certain behaviors—even helping animals to overcome traumatic experiences from their past. But there are also some things we just can't change—like a dog's basic design features.

When it doesn't appear that any balls were dropped by a perfectly good owner, we may look to the other polar extreme for an explanation—*nature*—assuming that the dog must be a "bad egg." Maybe there's something genetically *wrong* with him, like bad breeding or another identifiable disorder.

Looking through such a polarized lens, we're likely to completely miss the point. We are not seeing the dog for what and who he really is. The truth is, it's not nature *or* nurture. It's the interaction *between* nature and nurture. It's about the daily choices we make in handling and managing our dogs once we understand the instincts, capabilities, and limitations they bring to the table. One thing (nature) must work harmoniously with the other (nurture); this is the very essence of compatibility.

## Good Intentions

Dogs have been the practical companions to man for thousands of years. Since the dawn of civilization, humans have influenced and modified dog behavior for our own purposes, both individually and genetically. Through artificial selection—the deliberate reproduction of individuals with desirable characteristics—we designed master hunters, trackers, livestock guardians, herders, ratters, personal protectors, gladiators, lap warmers, and companions. If we needed a dog to help us track and hunt large game in sub-zero temperatures or a heat-hardy partner to move livestock over miles of plains, we designed exactly that. Exchanging one dog for the other—and operating on the assumption that one would work as well as another if trained and cared for in a certain way—would have resulted in unsuccessful hunts in the arctic and murdered livestock on the prairie.

Consider for a moment that this is precisely the situation we so often create with our approach to today's dogs, placing them in our homes as if they were interchangeable. We often assume that they all need similar amounts of exercise, affection, health care, and food in order to be suited to our lives.

When these dogs fail to live up to our expectations, the consequences can be serious for everyone. Personal and community safety are compromised when we unwittingly set them up for failure; and the dogs' lives are jeopardized when the owners give up. For all our good intentions, we continue to put a square dog in a round hole, and marvel at the consequences.

Behaviors that were highly desirable to our ancestors and were intentionally developed—such as killing small mammals and herding livestock—are now extremely problematic natural drives as they manifest in modern conditions.

We can all appreciate the inevitable consequences of asking a free-spirited, world-traveling human to settle down for a quiet life at a desk job. We know what happens when we try to change a person into someone they are not. Some terms are negotiable in a relationship, and some aren't. Of course you love your dog, but there is more. Whether that adorable long-eared dog at your feet is compatible with your own unique needs and limitations is the real question you need to ask yourself.

It *could* be a star-crossed love affair between a busy modern career woman and a cowboy hungering for the open range. What's more likely, however, is that you and your dog have come to a misunderstanding. You may simply need a good old-fashioned reality check in order to move forward.

As a modern dog lover, you most likely have never even had the opportunity to take a good honest look at your dog. This book can be that new pair of glasses that brings the details into focus for you, a crash course in dog science to prepare you for the dog love search and all of the many happy four-legged adventures ahead. You can navigate and enjoy a healthy relationship. You can, at last, *meet your dog.*

# CHAPTER ONE

# The Four Dog L.E.G.S.®

When we are selecting a dog or attempting to address specific behaviors with our existing canine partner, we need to be sure that we are looking at the whole animal. That way, we're less likely to miss something that might bite us later on; or, conversely, to give up prematurely when there may be a simple solution.

We don't want to fall in love if the relationship is inevitably doomed for failure. If we're asking a dog that is designed to be a protective guard to roll out the red carpet to anyone who walks in the door, or expecting a highly driven athlete to be a couch potato, everyone could end up frustrated.

Nor do we want to throw in the towel for the wrong reasons. What seems like an impossible situation may have a simple solution—maybe changing a daily routine or adjusting how we respond to the behavior we don't like. What seem to be irreconcilable differences may, in fact, just be basic misunderstandings. Remember that you and your dog are, after all, different types of animals.

In order to ensure that we don't misstep as we cross this bridge, we need a solid framework before we can make the connections. As we embark on this journey, we will benefit from using a basic system to help us account for all the moving parts of our dog's behavior. The L.E.G.S.® model—representing the four elements of Learning, Environment, Genetics, and Self—serves as a reliable and dynamic mechanism to guide us in our search for answers and solutions.

**LEARNING**—*your dog's experiences and education*

**ENVIRONMENT**—*the many aspects of your dog's external world*

**GENETICS**—*the DNA that designed your dog inside and out*

**SELF**—*the unique interior world of your dog: health, development, age, sex, and individuality*

## Dog L.E.G.S.®

After years of meeting dejected dog owners who couldn't understand their dogs' behaviors, it became my mission to help dogs and their people find a way to connect the dots. In 2009, I created the L.E.G.S.® system to organize the insights of dozens of scientific disciplines into something understandable for the modern dog owner. L.E.G.S.® is a simple framework for understanding the great range of factors that affect our dogs' behavior. It ensures that no stone goes unturned.

There is a wealth of scientific research out there about animals and nature; now we have to apply it to dogs. Stuck on the desks of academics and researchers, a great deal of the relevant science has for too long been out of reach of many dog owners. Well-established fields like evolutionary biology, applied behavior analysis, neurology, and ethology (and newer interdisciplinary fields such as epi-genetics, behavioral ecology, and neu-ro-ethology) all have their two cents to add to our understanding. There's no leap of logic in applying the natural sciences to our dogs; the remark-able thing is that we haven't done so already.

L.E.G.S.® accounts for all these elements that experts have discovered to be contributors to your dog's behavior; and it can help you easily under-stand the four fundamental parts that balance to make your dog tick.

**LEARNING:** Learning is the heartbeat of life's adaptation to ever-changing circumstances, and your dog is no exception to its influence. The incredi-ble truth is that your dog is taking notes *all the time*. Your habits, reactions, moods, friends, choices, routines, associations, and activities are all the subject of his unwavering scrutiny as a captive audience in your home with nothing better to do—and everything to gain from his attentiveness. The fact that you give Blakey that chewy treat to quiet him down every time he barks at the television has taught him to bark the moment you pick up the remote control so he can get his goody.

What your dog has learned about the consequences of his choices will affect his behavior in the future. What is pleasant and what is unpleasant? What matters to him and what makes no difference at all? What is the best way to get what he wants? What works for him?

Forget the notion of finding time to "train your dog." You are teaching him, and the world is teaching him, all day long in one big, dirty, mean-ingful experiment of trial and error. The only question is what he's actually learning. Everything sets a precedent for something else.

**ENVIRONMENT:** As for every species on earth, external conditions play a powerful role in the behavior a dog will express. We wouldn't put a hamster in a fish tank, and we can appreciate the inherent problems for an African lion trying to survive in the arctic tundra. We look at our dogs and struggle to understand what he could possibly be lacking. He's got it pretty good, right?

Just because our dog is our pet doesn't mean the concept of an appropriate habitat is irrelevant. We have all been unconsciously operating under those market-fed assumptions that "it's all how you raise 'em," that all dogs are just pets in different shapes and sizes. We haven't been told about their different designs and respective needs regarding habitat. The reality is that the details of the environment are just as important to a given dog as they would be for any other animal on the planet.

A wild animal lives in a certain ecosystem and has an ecological niche. He is perfectly suited to be exactly the way he is. This is because his design, physically and behaviorally, "worked" in prior generations that adapted to (yes, learned from) a specific environment. In nature, the environmental shoe has to fit the animal, and vice versa. When it doesn't fit, the animal is stressed, behaves strangely, and struggles to survive. Nature and men have selected dogs for a variety of behaviors and habitats. Most of them bear little resemblance to the pet dog life.

So if your Border Collie is pacing and whining in your new apartment like a caged animal in a zoo, consider for a moment that it might be an ill-suited habitat that has caused this behavior. If his ancestors spent eighteen hours a day in the field and he spends twenty-three hours a day indoors, his cnvironment may be his problem.

**GENETICS:** Genes are the instructions for life and survival, passed from one generation to the next. They determine the reasonable scope of what an animal can and can't do. Genetics also provides room for change and adjusting to circumstances.

The shape of a dog—his size, body, ears, nose, fur, tail, and even behavior—is the product of selected genes intended to promote specific behaviors within specific environments. Dogs look so different from each other because they *are* so different from each other. The physical forms of almost every breed of dog—their varied sizes, structures, and characteristics—arose as the direct result of their being purposefully selected for the behaviors they expressed. The great changes to form followed the function—and the two were always (and still are) inseparable.

Breeding just for looks is pretty much a modern phenomenon; and it still doesn't get us away from the behavioral traits that are connected to the physical features. All dogs are just not created equal. A St. Bernard will not beat a Siberian Husky in sled racing; and a Toy Poodle will not take down a wild boar—no matter what kind of training you do.

We can't expect a dog to behave in ways he was not genetically prepared to behave. Your Fox Terrier is just following instructions when he chases and kills a rabbit in the yard. Despite your repeated scolding, he is not being "bad" or "disobedient." He is just being a terrier with a genetically intact predatory sequence aimed at killing small mammals.

Other kinds of dogs were genetically selected only to display part of this predatory sequence, and some were bred to display virtually no predatory behavior whatsoever. Needless to say, these historically-based differences in your dog's DNA are going to matter a great deal (at least to that rabbit).

While you don't need to be a whiz at the hundreds of dog breeds out there, you do need to know which of the ten genetically distinct working groups your dog belongs to. You need to know what kind of job your dog was born to do. You need to know if he is a *natural dog*, a *sight hound*, a *guardian*, a *toy dog*, a *scent hound*, a *gun dog*, a *terrier*, a *bull dog*, a *herding dog*, or a *world dog*. Your understanding about his historical purpose—how he was purposefully bred to behave in certain ways—is important to success in your relationship. We need to use our dog's genetics as a practical point of reference for our expectations about their behavior.

SELF: Self, the last pillar of L.E.G.S.®, is inherently the most ambiguous, as it describes the internal factors that are unique to each individual dog. Age, sex, health, disease, disability, nutrition, stress levels, and personal quirks will all play an important part in your dog's behavior.

Some of these aspects of the self are obvious. Your female puppy is unlikely to have the problem of lifting her leg to urinate on the sofa, while an intact adult male is extremely likely to exhibit this kind of behavior. A deaf dog is less likely to come when called than one with sharp hearing. And a starving animal is more likely than a well-fed one to guard his food bowl aggressively.

There are times, however, when the effects of the self are more subtle. Often a veterinarian becomes an essential player in these cases, performing tests and helping your dog compensate for physical problems. For example, you might not have realized that Ellie was feeling pain in her hips these past few months; you only noticed that she'd become defensive when your other collie walked by her bed.

Some behaviors are normal and appropriate to sex, age, and development, while others may indicate serious cause for concern. Knowing what to expect as a dog develops, matures, and ages can provide great relief. Your trusted vet will become a critical adviser for you throughout the course of your dog's life, explaining how everything from fear periods to adolescence to old age can affect your canine friend.

There is another aspect of the self, one that in many ways owns the heart of our emotional connection to our dogs. Like us, your dog is ultimately a one-in-a-million individual creature filled with likes and dislikes that make her unique and special. She likes the peanut butter treats and hates the cheese bites. She curls up in the nook behind your knees when you sleep. She always spins twice before she poops. She loves the spot on the back of the couch by the window. She licks your tears when you cry. She is *your* dog.

## Dog L.E.G.S.® in Action

Understanding the four pillars of L.E.G.S.®, and how each one affects your dog, will help you arrive at the root cause of behavior problems and allow you to make an informed decision about what your dog truly needs.

Consider Adam's story as it illustrates the four aspects of L.E.G.S.®. The lettered annotations within his story represent each pillar of L.E.G.S.® as events unfolded for him and his dog.

Adam was a second-year college student (E) I met at my behavior center a few years ago. Adam didn't realize what he would be facing when he adopted Donut, a two-year-old female (S) Plott Hound (G). He'd been told that Donut was housebroken (L), knew the "sit" command (L), and had a fear of bicycles (L). He had no idea that she would have a hard time living in his small apartment in an urban neighborhood in Asheville's historic district (E). He didn't know she had a voice that echoed for miles (G), or that she would sing all day (G) while his two neighbors who worked nights tried to sleep (E). Adam did not realize that Donut needed five miles a day of running exercise (G) to keep her from eating the furniture, and that once he started working on his thesis, walks longer than twenty minutes would be impossible (E).

All he saw at the shelter were her big brown eyes (S) and her trembling body at the back of her cage. He melted like an ice cube in summer. Adam felt her soft ears and the way she nestled under his arm (S), and that was it. Not for an instant did he imagine it would be a struggle for Donut to share space with his roommate's old cat (E) without incessantly barking and chasing it (G). He didn't know that her raccoon-hunting instincts might transfer over to the tabby. He also had no idea that Donut was a highly skilled escape artist (L) who would bolt out the front door any chance she got as college buddies came in and out unannounced (E), and that he would spend hours chasing her around the block as she gleefully frightened the neighbors (G). He wasn't prepared when Animal Control came to his apartment and cited Donut as a dangerous animal in the community (E). When adopting her, Adam knew she had some allergies that would require medication (S), but he didn't budget for the lawsuit and behaviorist. He just fell in love with her.

Had Adam known about Donut's L.E.G.S.®—or if someone at the shelter had been able to explain what he was signing up for as an apartment-dwelling college student adopting a scent hound, or if his vet had discussed Donut's design characteristics on his initial visit—Adam might have decided that Donut was the wrong dog for his current lifestyle. Or he might have been smitten enough to set a different schedule before adopting her, and rent a different house—one with a big fenced yard, no roommate's cat, and no nearby neighbors to complain about the noise and feline rodeos.

Maybe Donut was a love that just wasn't meant to be. Or maybe Adam could have been better prepared and taken preventive measures to ensure success with his new dog, given some compassionate and practical guidance. But Adam didn't have the information and tools that he needed. When threatened with legal action, he felt he had no choice; and so, heartbroken, he returned Donut to the shelter.

## Dog L.E.G.S.® for You

It doesn't have to end this way for you and your dog. In this book, each element of your dog's L.E.G.S.® will be examined and explained in gritty, real-life detail by a practicing dog behavior consultant (think: mixed-species family therapist) who understands how and why life with your dog is not always easy. Over fifteen years of mediating relationships between people and their dogs from the integrated perspective of applied ethology (the study of the intersection of animal and human behavior regarding captive and domesticated species) has made me a compassionate and realistic friend to thousands of clients seeking solace in their homes.

Every year I learn more from research, colleagues, and my clients and their dogs as I apply these principles and observe their effects. I want to share what I've learned. I want to share the science that makes a difference in the lives of my clients and their dogs with the millions of dog lovers who want that newfound healthy relationship, too.

# CHAPTER TWO

# Learning

In any relationship, both parties bring their past experiences to the table. No one—including your dog—is immune to baggage and habits from years gone by. Every individual is shaped, profoundly and often unconsciously, by what he or she has learned in life. Moments become memories, and memories become ideas. Certain actions pay off and become useful strategies that, over time, become habitual responses. Life provides a million opportunities for some kind of take-home message for your dog.

What will the message of the moment be for your dog? Is it that first monumental discovery that the appearance of the leash may mean a walk is coming? When you sit down at your computer, does that indicate a great opportunity to eat cat poop out of the litterbox? Maybe a mental note that small children are grabby and have little regard for personal space? The possibility that biting your pant legs when you walk through the house is the best way to get you to throw the ball for her? That little fuzzy, doe-eyed cutie at your feet is a whole lot smarter than you may be giving her credit for. Her memory is remarkable, and she is taking notes 24-7.

Since learning arguably provides the greatest window of opportunity for change and adjustment in your dog's behavior, it is important that you understand how your dog learns on a practical, day-to-day level. In this chapter, you will be introduced to this critically important element of your canine partner's behavior. You will learn to recognize your part in shaping her adorable little rituals as well as those irritating cycles of misbehavior. This will prevent you from projecting false motives onto her and becoming unnecessarily resentful about her sock stealing and kid chasing. You will see how events can take on strong meanings for your dog, however random her associations may seem (people wearing white coats don't necessarily have sharp objects in their pockets just because the vet does; and the sound of the cupboard door opening doesn't always mean she gets a treat).

## Dog Learning vs. Dog Training

If I had a dollar for every time a wife sarcastically asked me if I could also train her husband at the same time as their dog, I would be a very rich woman. The thought of taking someone who is driving us crazy to be "trained" and getting them back as a cooperative, pleasant replacement who no longer exhibits those annoying behaviors is appealing indeed.

Many people come into therapy with their dog (or with any partner, for that matter) with the goal of fixing or controlling unwanted behavior. But the reality is that all relationships are a two-way street, even when it appears that one party has the upper hand or that one is inherently more dependent on the other. Between you and your dog, there are two individuals trying to negotiate life in harmony. No one is "bad" for failing to align with the other's expectations. No one is in service to the other.

A common misperception is that a dog's learning is simply about "training." If only it were as simple as attending a six-week obedience class and emerging with the perfect pet. Here is a big pill to swallow before we begin our conversation about learning: *"Dog training" is a misnomer.* Your canine pal is no more "trainable" than your spouse. What dogs and spouses *are* is teachable by life, and you are obviously an important part of life's experiences in both cases. Under the right set of circumstances, and with the right set of tools, learning can be easily guided. But there are also limitations and ethical constraints in light of the fact that your dog is having her *own* life experience. She is not a minion.

She might follow you from room to room and literally lick your feet, but that does not mean your dog is at your beck and call. Yes, she will look at you "that way," and it is really tempting to think that she's solely interested in doing what makes you happy. But that sincere look you see in her eyes after she's committed a crime is just a creative strategy of making good with the boss so that things work out in her favor. We can call it an apology, but your little puppy is just instinctively—and logically—stacking that deck. Her appeasing gestures that look like fawning have another function: they trigger cascades of a satisfying chemical called oxytocin to promote bonding and reduce aggression—in both of you. She's getting trained, all right. She's doing the math that will add up to better results for her.

You *do* make a great difference in your dog's learning. You are providing her with on-the-job training for this "pet" gig every day. But make no mistake: *Life is the great trainer;* it's not you. What you want her to learn is not necessarily what she will learn. You cannot simply program her according to your wishes.

You can and should, however, provide learning experiences that will influence her behavior. You are the one with the opposable thumbs, upright posture, and bigger brain. These things give you the ability to navigate a modern life filled with doors, latches, cars, and money for the family. Because of this, you do have to be the one taking the lead—not unlike how a parent does for their child. She is simply not equipped to navigate the restrictions and demands of a pet life and make good decisions on her own. She needs you to be proactive. Though you should work diligently to create as many appropriate opportunities as possible for her to make choices and have control, there will be many circumstances in which her own ideas could get her into big trouble.

Learning is not an event; it is a constant process, and it is your responsibility to foster experiences that will be beneficial to her perpetual learning. Each of those small mental notes she takes (*"coming" to you when you call from the bathroom is a bad idea because you only call her in there when it is doggy bath time*) and every big learning moment (*particularly the traumatic ones in which her very life seems to be in danger*) can deeply influence her perceptions and reactions down the road. She needs you to help her to make sense of it all.

## The "Good" Dog

When you think of all the things you have read about dog training and behavior, all the advice you have ever sought (or been given against your will, whether by neighbors on morning walks or the in-laws on holiday visits), what does the conversation usually revolve around? People endlessly debate how to "teach a dog who is boss"; whether one can "teach an old dog new tricks"; the best way to "teach him not to jump"; and which "training methods" are best. We've been taught to believe that, with the right techniques and enough determination, we can almost train a fish to fly or a bird to swim.

While we chase the elusive holy grail of dog training techniques that will finally solve all of our problems and make our dog "good," we are missing more obvious and commonsense facts right under our noses. We often fail to notice the real conditions that make "obedience" to our directions impossible, and end up punishing the dog for what is out of his control. The dog fails because we are unwittingly neglecting certain factors influencing his behavior. We get frustrated and embarrassed as the neighbors look on, feeling that we are being judged for not being able to control our dog. This is because we have been taught to believe many silly cultural myths about the way our dog learns.

# Three Useless Myths about the "Good" Dog

♥ **MYTH #1: There is a magic dog training method. We just have to find it, so we can have a "good" dog!**

That magic method doesn't exist. There are plenty of good ideas and practices in dog training, but there's no magic recipe to follow that will yield the perfectly well behaved dog no matter what. Bummer.

Dog trainers have done little over the years to dispel the idea of a perfect training routine. As a matter of fact, virtually the entire dog training industry revolves around claims and debates about assertions of exactly this idea—that there is a magic wand that can be used to train all dogs, and so-and-so finally found it. An eager, often desperate, public is looking for a quick fix.

When training—"It's all how you raise them"—fails, the trainer usually tells the client that there is something wrong with the dog or its owner (the fallback myth of a "bad dog" or "bad owner"). Like any other relationship, our relationship with our dog is complicated by a series of factors that all need to be considered. As you now know, learning does not happen in a vacuum; it is vitally connected to environment, genetics, and self.

If Rascal the Jack Russell terrier has been grabbing Fluffy the hamster, leash corrections or promised treats for leaving Fluffy alone are unlikely to prevent Rascal from killing the hamster. This is because (a) Rascal's ancestors have been prized ratters for four generations and (b) Rascal has access to Fluffy's cage. Rascal simply finds himself subject to the powerful influence of his DNA as it overrides all logical thought when he encounters little Fluffy. Training really has nothing to do with it.

♥ **MYTH #2: We have to be the "alpha dog." Once we put the dog in his place, he will respect us and be "good."**

Spoiler alert: Our dog knows we are not a dog. Lizards know we are not a lizard, and birds know we're not a bird. Imitating the ritualized behaviors of wolves or dogs does not convince them that we speak their language. You can't fool or dominate them through awkward "alpha rolls," "nose grabs," "scruff shakes," and "bites." (Yes, I've actually had clients who bite their dogs because someone convinced them it was a good idea.) Your dog *may* walk away with a new impression of you if you try these techniques, but it won't be favorable. You'll just end up with a bite on the arm or a mouthful of fur.

Some people claim that being the leader of the pack is everything, and that one must confidently engage, win every battle of wills, and establish control. The truth is this: Scientifically, dominance is about *control of resources, not control of the other*. We have effectively confused the idea of dominance with that of being domineering. There's a really big difference. Bullies are domineering because they have something to prove. Leaders are dominant because they are already in control of the situation, i.e., the environment—and that motivates others to get on board.

When we control the dog's access to resources that matter to him (e.g., doors opening to the exciting world, food bowls being filled, attention being lavished, balls being thrown), we are being a kind of "key master"—possessing the ability to access everything. That said, most of us don't intentionally control these things every time; they tend to just happen without us thinking much about it. So we must consider our dog's perception of these events. A hundred times a day, our dog can perceive us *either* as a doting servant jumping to meet his every need *or* as a respectable manager of events. It's better to be seen as the latter.

When we teach our dog to "ask" for things by offering a behavior like sitting, it instills in him that we are the management. It also creates structure that can reduce anxiety and increase confidence. Plus, like children who use "please" and "thank you" to get what they want, a dog with such etiquette is remarkably more pleasant to live with. When there is an atmosphere in the relationship of order and cooperation for all of the little things, the stage has been set for adherence to instructions when it really counts. Forget intimidation and threats. You won't need them. Altercations, power struggles, and physical battles are a complete waste of time.

💜 **MYTH #3: A "good" dog likes everybody, wants to meet everybody, and wants every person to pet him and every dog to sniff him.**

This one really drives me nuts. Dogs are not politicians running for office. They did not sign up to kiss every baby and shake every hand. Why should dogs be expected to enjoy being touched and petted by total strangers? Imagine how you would feel if you walked down the block with your spouse, and a group of strangers said "Ooo, she is pretty! Can I pet her?" and your spouse said, "Sure!" and invited them to stroke and kiss you. I wouldn't know who to slug first in this situation—the strangers or my husband! But this is exactly what we do to our dogs, standing in awe when they finally bite the tenth guy that we have allowed to fondle a complete stranger.

While some dogs do enjoy interacting with virtually anyone, *most* dogs don't. When they tell us, through their body language, growling or snapping, they're often reprimanded or punished for being a "bad" dog. It is our job to know our dogs, what they like, and what they are comfortable with. It is our job to protect their personal space from invasion by strangers without justification, explanation, or guidance.

Similarly, when it comes to encountering other *dogs*, if we keep insisting that they socialize with every canine on the street, we should not wonder why it keeps blowing up in our face. We may think that all dogs should stop and sniff each other or play. We might force the issue by warning, "Say hello," or "Be nice," when our dog hides behind our legs or lunges, barking *Go away!* at the big Labrador coming straight for him

with outstretched arms. We wouldn't make our children meet every child they encounter in public, so why would we force our dog to greet every new "friend" we see? It's unfair, and we shouldn't be surprised if some dogs behave aggressively or defensively in response to such social flooding.

There's a lot to be said for minding our own business while holding out the possibility that every now and then, there will be someone really worth meeting. We would be wise to provide our dogs with selective social opportunities where there are context-relevant interactions with people and animals, rather than adopt a free-for-all approach to socialization. While some dogs are natural socialites, a great many of them prefer to casually enjoy their walks with their loved ones and only passively smell and observe their human and canine compatriots from a safe distance as they go by.

## The Common Sense of Learning

Life is complicated. There's a lot to figure out about getting through it, and things are always changing. Learning is how we keep up. For animals, including pets, the evolutionary purpose of learning is to provide the best chance of survival in a world filled with both predictable patterns and constant changes. Learning does not happen *despite* conditions. Learning happens *within* conditions, and even directly *because of* conditions. Learning is also inextricably linked to the other elements of L.E.G.S.®

Lessons do not benefit only the learner. The really important stuff learned, over time, becomes evolutionary "family wisdom" carried through DNA, as offspring are born "knowing" what to do in a variety of important circumstances. An animal's forebears learn critical lessons that genetically prepare them for a new generation of learners, as significant experiences can literally change the information passed on to their offspring. Those new student animals in turn discover if the shoe still fits in their ever-changing environment. In this way, the past serves as a genetic "user manual" to guide the animal's understanding of how things work. And that user manual is constantly modified and improved for future reference and subsequent generations.

Recognizing and adapting to meaningful conditions is the essence of the learning process. The truly beneficial strategies and most meaningful experiences leave their mark on the genetic information that gets passed on. Evolution may happen over generations in a given animal's heritage, but it happens in just one little moment—of trial and error, of success or failure, of critical discernment—at a time. Genes learn how to best win at the game of life through individuals.

When it comes to our own canine companion, what he learns may not have the chance to affect future generations (we have probably prevented that with a neutering procedure). Nonetheless, it's really powerful stuff. Learning keeps all the elements of L.E.G.S.® moving in real time, giving you and your dog the ability to shift with the turning tides.

# Thinking Clearly

When your dog becomes stimulated—be it excited or terrified (good or bad excitement is pretty much the same event to the body)—her nervous system gets stressed. As the level of stimulation/stress in her body increases and builds toward the fight or flight survival response, logical thinking and decision making abilities go down. It is really important to consider how your dog's internal conditions (self) are influencing her ability to pay attention, follow directions, and learn. If the dog is overstimulated, amped up, frightened, or stressed, she may act in ways that surprise, annoy, or concern you. If she remains in an elevated state of stress (distress) or has a traumatic experience, her ability to learn can become additionally compromised. Remember to pause and consider this possibility, and observe your dog for signs of stress and excessive excitement as you try to make sense of her behavior.

## Puppyhood—Where It All Begins

First impressions are everything. Nature has installed a special period of development in young animals to prepare them for the road ahead. During puppyhood, dogs are especially sensitive and open to learning from their experiences. The lessons an animal (including your dog) learns at this phase will set the stage for his future perceptions and behaviors in a powerful way.

By about 16 weeks of age, your puppy will have reached the end of his critical socialization period. You don't always get the chance to raise your own dog and influence his experience during this time. You may have some knowledge of what his life was like during those first few months, or it could be a complete mystery. If you do acquire your puppy before he reaches four months of age, you have a precious opportunity to cultivate positive experiences and a healthy relationship from the start.

This period of time is a really big deal. This critical socialization period programs an animal for life, teaching him the basics: who his friends and enemies are, what is safe and what is dangerous, what is normal and what is weird, what to do and what not to do, in all kinds of conditions. Puppies are like sponges during this time. What your dog experiences—and what he doesn't—during these months can create enormous behavior problems in the future or go a long way toward preventing them. Having positive or neutral experiences with something can prevent fearful reactions to it later in life. Though not the only factor, "how you raise them" does make one heck of a difference.

When you raise your own dog, you can take steps to ensure that he has positive, constructive, educational experiences at this age that prepare him to confidently and appropriately handle a variety of situations. You want to buffer against potential problems by *deliberately educating your dog about the conditions that are most likely to present the greatest challenges for him.*

Taking into consideration all four elements of L.E.G.S.®, think about what conditions (environment) your puppy is being exposed to moment to moment, and how he might have been designed to react to those conditions (genetics). You can deliberately work with him, teaching him (learning) how to handle potentially challenging circumstances at this opportune time in his life and development (self). The goal is to get one up on Mother Nature, not wait for instincts to kick in. This critical period gives us the largest window you will ever have in your dog's life to use learning to compete with the less flexible influences of genetics and the unpredictable and complex nature of the environment. An ounce of prevention, as they say, is worth a pound of cure.

## Meaning and Baggage

What does it all *mean*? Ah, the quintessential question of scholars, poets, philosophers, and the sentimental throughout history. We poor humans agonize endlessly in our own minds, to friends, and in therapy to understand the meaning of events in our past, the behaviors of others, and even our own thoughts. We desperately try to organize the experiences we are having, attempting to make sense of it all.

We look over at our dogs enviously. They are so lucky. They don't have to deal with all of this stuff. They don't ask themselves what it all *means*. Or do they?

Your spaniel may not experience the onslaught of life events in the same way you do, but she is indeed constantly working to make sense of both big and small stuff in life that seems important to her. It's not that your dog is contemplating her purpose in the universe as she peers out the window at the sunrise. But the need to discover meaning in one's world— as well as the resulting acquisition or abandonment of certain ideas about that world—is a fundamental characteristic of every living being. Your dog is no exception.

What does it mean when you yell and stomp around the house holding a small black box to your ear? You don't seem to be going anywhere, and there doesn't appear to be any threat outside the house, but clearly something is wrong!? When you act this way, it can make your dog want to run away. He lowers his head and approaches you with tail slowly wagging, reading your face for signs of approval. Is it safe to be near you? Has he done something wrong? When he lifts his head under your hand and you shoo him away, he is frightened. Maybe sitting next to you when you are on the couch is a bad thing? He is so confused, trying to make sense of your actions. What does it all *mean* for him?

Just like us, our dogs are paying attention to what is happening around them all the time. They are reading the signals in order to determine what, if any, meaning those signals have for them and their well-being. From the moment of birth, all of us animals are interpreting the world around us for clues. *What is that? Is this thing dangerous? Can I eat it? Does he like me? Is this event noteworthy? How does this relate to that?*

Every time an animal makes a mental note about the meaning of something (angry owner with scowling face = dangerous to approach for petting), the brain is organizing information about the world into that which matters and that which does not, categorizing the event for future reference. This process of adding, sorting, or changing meaning is known in behavioral science as *classical conditioning*. Traditional behaviorists call an inherited meaning you were born with an *unconditioned stimulus* and a new one you pick up along the way a *conditioned stimulus*.

Russian physiologist Ivan Pavlov illuminated this process for the scientific community when he conditioned a dog to salivate in response to the sound of a bell that routinely predicted the presentation of food. He made a previously meaningless bell meaningful to the dog because he created a pattern between a random event and a really important one. The bell became something to pay attention to, when it had previously been meaningless to the dog.

This kind of learning by association happens in life all the time, outside of Pavlov's laboratory. We flinch when something is thrown at our face, and feel queasy when we drive by the diner where we ate bad fish that time. We drool like Pavlov's dog when we see the golden arches from the interstate as our stomach rumbles on a long road trip. The clinking sound of the leash being picked up wakes your dog from a dead sleep and readies her for adventure. You open a crinkly bag in the kitchen, and she is suddenly sitting at your feet. You pick up the nail trimmer, and she runs under the bed. These once-innocuous signals have taken on meaning because they relate to something else that is meaningful. And yet the new flowers on the kitchen table, or the beautiful dress you just put on for your date, or even the fact that you're busy working on your résumé don't seem to register at all to her. Why?

Nature is very efficient. There are not just dozens but literally millions of things happening inside and around us at any given moment. While some require our attention or a response, the vast majority of occurrences in the world around us must simply go by unnoticed. No creature can respond to every sight, smell, and sound in the world; any animal would die of neurological exhaustion if it did. So nature has filters, and it's constantly improving them to help us sift through and sort things into categories

# How to Change Your Dog's Mind about Something

If your dog has an idea that something is "bad" and you want to change it to "good," try pairing up the unfavorable event with his favorite thing. If he despises your uncle Ron and worships the tennis ball, make Ron = tennis ball. If the ball only appears when Ron comes over, and lives on the shelf until he does, your dog will be hard-pressed to hate Ron as much as he used to. He may not want to be Ron's best friend, but maybe he will at least play fetch with you while Ron is there instead of running into the bedroom.

without wasting precious time and energy on irrelevant information. It's kind of like Google for the brain.

The process of filtering and organizing sounds, sights, smells, and other events is largely unconscious, running deep into the psyche as a basic mechanism of survival for even the simplest of creatures. Critical to the primal survival of even the simplest organisms, this kind of learning in action is often referred to as *lizard brain*.

From toads to tigers, the identification of meaning in the environment motivates the animal to pay attention, potentially pursue opportunities, and avoid imminent danger. Rudimentary, reflexive, emotional, and largely unconscious, these classically conditioned responses help us to read the map of life and respond in ways that help us live to see another day. The search for and discovery of meaning in life is the basis of our ideas about the world, and plays a critical role in setting the stage for all of our reactions and behaviors.

**GENETIC MEANING:** All creatures are designed to reflexively respond to certain sights, sounds, smells, sensations, and events as meaningful, while completely ignoring the rest of them. Our bodies and brains "remember" what our ancestors learned about the meanings of certain things.

Your dog naturally notices the scampering of squirrels in the yard, the expressions of emotion on your face, and the smells inside your garbage can. He ignores the new red flowers you planted that the hummingbirds are obsessed with, the acorns in the yard the squirrels have been so busy collecting, and the stack of bills on the table that's totally stressing you out.

Your dog also learns from his own experiences, and is taking notes about the meaning of the world around him for the benefit of his potential offspring. He doesn't consciously know when this is happening, of course. For example, after he was attacked by a bear last year on that camping trip, he began to relate the smell of a bear with life-threatening danger. He didn't consciously make a note for his future descendants, but he did note that bear smell = bad. The trauma associated with that smell could actually change his DNA and prime his descendants to be fearful of and actively avoid the smell. So this type of experience does not necessarily end with him. If he were to reproduce, the message about the bear smell could be passed on to his offspring. It's a recently understood natural event called "epi-genetic inheritance," and it's the best proof we've ever had that learning is an evolutionary event.[1]

Modern epi-geneticists have discovered that these experiences can leave epi-genetic "tags," which actually reprogram the animal's DNA. [2] The exciting new interdisciplinary field of neuro-ethology takes an in-depth look at how animals have come, over the course of many years, to recognize the meaning of important information in their environments on a neurological level, and how that data is stored and passed on in order to modify the behavioral and even physical shape of future generations as a result. We are really starting to understand, as science continues to shed light on these processes, how capable all species are of adapting their senses, bodies, and behaviors to automatically respond to signals in their environment that are meaningful to their survival. As the world changes, each generation is given the chance to add their own two cents to the user manual for a species and family. The genetic software is endlessly being updated for better performance in the future.

CONDITIONAL MEANING: Because the world is constantly changing (often extremely, from one moment to the next), animals have to be primed to roll with the punches. Information that might have been relevant five minutes ago (*i.e., the placement of the bowl on the floor elicits salivation because it means that it is time to eat!*) could suddenly be totally unimportant because a condition has shifted (*the scent drifting through the open window of a bear in the nearby woods elicits instant fear and means it's not safe to eat now*). When it comes to meaning, the truth is that learned associations are never static in real life. What something actually means in a given moment always depends on the circumstances. How it is perceived, and even whether it is perceived at all, depends on the greater context it occurs in. Meanings, like everything else, do not exist in a vacuum.

The treat you gave your dog this morning for doing his little dance in the kitchen had good associations for him as he gobbled it up. That same treat caused him to run away from you when you offered it later to try to lure him into the bathtub. He's no fool. He can see the towel and shampoo bottle in your other hand and he knows what *that* means. Suddenly that chicken jerky you are holding reeks of a mean trick. The circumstances around a stimulus changed, so the meaning of that stimulus in the moment changed for him as well.

The signals in your dog's world are being perpetually reprioritized and reorganized in this manner depending on the conditions of her internal self and external environment. The meaning of something can shift in an instant—often dramatically—depending on her age, health, stress level, weather, relationships, and thousands of other circumstances.

It's not just this way for dogs; it's equally true for any animal on earth. In Africa, for example, lions eat zebras on a regular basis; and the sight of these four-legged, black and white striped equines usually signals a specific action for a lion: hunt; eat. But not always.

Imagine, for a moment, a young lion approaches a watering hole to find a herd of zebra drinking from the same hole. The lion has a learned response (genetically and very likely, from his own experience) to the sight of a zebra. Few things are more meaningful to a hungry lion than an easy meal. But let's also say that there has been a recent drought, and the lion has traveled for miles in search of water. In this instance, even the strong association of zebra and food is subject to conditions. The circumstances of the dry season (environment) have caused the lion to prioritize the desire for water over the desire for food. For now, the sight of that baby zebra straying from its mother is of little interest. The more important element to the lion is the water. The meaning of something deeply ingrained can be changed in an instant when the conditions warrant it.

It might just be survival economics, but this it-depends-on-the-circumstances business can be really frustrating when you're screaming "Come!" repeatedly to your dog as he ignores you in pursuit of the jogger. A moment ago he was responding beautifully as you practiced his new command in the front yard. It all changed when the guy ran past the house. Now you'd think Tonka had never heard the word before.

Meaning, like everything else, is not static. It's no personal insult to you when your boyfriend fails to hear a word you have said about your horrible day when the big game is on. Likewise, your dog is usually just going about his business, merrily searching for rabbit poop in the leaves, when you call him desperately to come back inside. When any partner ignores you, it doesn't necessarily indicate that you are unloved or no longer meaningful to them. It just means that, at least for that moment, the lizard brain has filtered you out for something more important. He still loves you, even as he chases the jogger down the street.

Your own deep quest for meaning in life (and that arguably simpler search that your dog is on) is just classical conditioning at work for the benefit of survival. Baggage, it turns out, has an evolutionary purpose: to keep us all safe, sound, well-fed, and productive in the world. It's not nearly as personal as we make it out to be. Just the recognition of this universal process can save any relationship a great deal of unnecessary misunderstanding.

# Meaning and L.E.G.S.® in Action

## ♥ Learning

Events that trigger a strong fear response are likely to create a new association to whatever signals your dog perceived in that event (these experiences are stored to long-term memory immediately). Any number of otherwise neutral things can become "bad" to your dog if something scary happens at the exact moment the sight, sound, or smell is perceived. This is why the use of pain or threats in training is like playing Russian roulette with your dog's behavior. Even if just coincidental, he might pair up a random smell or sight as related to the scary or painful event. He might develop a superstitious fear of water bottles because he got squirted for barking too much. He could run and hide under the bed when the doorbell rings because he was chastised one time a little too harshly for jumping up on your guest. Assuming he will associate his "crime" with the "punishment" is a mistake, when any number of signals in the environment could randomly get paired up with the "bad" thing. It's important that you remember how scary things can create a powerful negative reaction in the future.

## ♥ Environment

Your dog's environment changes moment to moment, and his responses to sensory cues (and your cues) will depend on what is happening around him. What is meaningful in one set of circumstances is not meaningful in another; the environment sets the limitations and possibilities for learning. Sometimes your efforts at change will be swimming against the tide because the environment is constantly reinforcing the original idea. For example, in a home where a man is threatening to your dog, it is futile to try to teach the dog to not be scared of men.

## ♥ Genetics

Your dog is genetically wired to find things like garbage, your lunch, poop, and other animal scents, including olfactory cues like those from hormones, as potentially meaningful opportunities. He is also instinctually conditioned to recognize certain events as threatening. People frequently trigger defensive behavior from dogs by accident. A few common examples are leaning over an unfamiliar dog to deliver a hug, or trying to retrieve the steak back from the clutches of his mouth after he swipes it from our plate. These actions make sense to us, but they can have totally different meanings to your dog. We are unaware of any reflexive reaction we might trigger from the dog in response to what he perceives as a threat to his personal space or his yummy prize. Depending on his genetic group, your dog might also find fast-moving objects, small mammals, the presence of a predator, or large game particularly meaningful—or, in contrast, not meaningful at all.

## ♥ Self

What your dog experiences as meaningful will change as he develops (sexually mature male dogs find certain hormonal smells very meaningful, whereas immature female puppies would filter them out). Your dog's health will also affect the acquisition or loss of meaning ascribed to a certain event (the favorite ball that he spent hours a day chasing might suddenly become invisible to him when he is sick). When he's older and experiences some loss of cognitive function, he might not recognize the difference between the carpet and the pee pads anymore. Throughout the course of his life, your dog's internal state plays a powerful role.

## Trial and Error

We all make mistakes. The big question, cliché as it may be, is whether or not we learn from them. Do we do the same thing over and over again, even though it doesn't work out for us? Or do we make different choices and modify our behavior in order to get a better outcome? Surely we can all change, right? Learning from the consequences of one's actions enables every creature to adapt to life.

Failure to learn is a death sentence in the game of survival. Nature designed us to do what works, and to stop doing things that don't work. This kind of *operant learning*—learning by the consequences of our actions—is a fundamental tool of adaptation.

If it's so fundamental, why the heck can't our eighty-pound black lab get the hang of it and stop jumping all over the cable guy? Heaven knows we have punished him enough for doing it, yelling and jerking in admonishment as he leaps with abandon at every visiting victim that enters our home. We have rewarded him with cookies for sitting ad nauseam, yet he continues to pounce all over the company—though he now periodically sits down and looks to us to deliver a snack in between jumps. How many mistakes does a dog have to make to learn a lesson?

There are two main reasons to consider when answering this question. The first is this: he is not making a mistake—jumping totally works for him. He is getting exactly what he was after—attention—so your reaction to his jumping is actually rewarding him, thus reinforcing the behavior. We rarely look at our dog's behavior this logically. We scold, or try to distract and bribe. We try to change his motivation rather than try to understand that motivation more fully. If we unrealistically expect our human and doggie counterparts to just "be good," rather than to exert their own free will and behave according to their best interests, we may be missing some pretty critical pieces of the puzzle. If we walk away feeling completely disappointed in them, we may have misunderstood their behavior.

The second reason is more complicated, and has to do with unconscious behavior versus conscious behavior. The truth is that actions are not always as deliberate as they might seem. In fact, some decisions are not really decisions at all.

Sometimes we act very deliberately to accomplish a goal. Other times, we have no earthly idea why we behave as we do; we find ourselves repeating behaviors we would prefer to stop. But there are powerful natural forces underlying all of our actions, and we are not always in control of them despite our ability to reason and solve problems. Having a realistic grasp of a person or an animal's ability to change is critical to the success of that relationship. Some habits run very, very deep.

History is the best yardstick for judging the ability to modify behavior. It tells us just how long we may expect the learning curve to be. The longer a behavior has been effective for an individual, the more resistant she will be to changing this pattern in the future. This is why nobody—human or dog—escapes a therapist's office without digging into family history; how far back a habit goes really makes a difference in potential outcomes.

Sometimes the consequence of an action is extremely favorable not only for one individual, but for generations of individuals. In this case, the habit has been literally embedded in the genetics of the animal and thus has the power to motivate behavior even as it continues to fail or be punished. Such a behavioral survival strategy has become an *impulse—a modal action pattern*—that is automatic and self-reinforcing (even chemically rewarding the animal with a dopamine release in the brain for engaging in the behavior). It is largely unconscious and unintentional.

For example: a natural predator may continue to hunt when an opportunity presents itself, long after he has learned that food will be provided for him in captivity. For a tiger in a zoo or a Husky in the suburbs, the free meals we humans offer do not erase the powerful, subconscious impetus to respond to fast-moving prey. The rewards that resulted from this behavior in their predecessors reinforced and literally shaped their DNA to respond. This kind of reinforcement history has such staying power in the biology of the learner that it can persevere, despite changing conditions in the environment, for a very long time.

So unless there are some seriously sufficient competing motivations—strong enough to rearrange the priorities in the moment by rendering the hunt suddenly too dangerous or secondary to some other survival demand—*the modal action patterns* will just emerge without a thought. And once again, the animal will enjoy the cascade of dopamine surging through its system, reinforcing the behavior further.

Your black lab's little jumping habit is fueled by more than the attention everyone keeps feeding him for doing it; it is also a behavior that has worked out really well for friendly, solicitous pups greeting their buddies for thousands of years.

While humans are sometimes able to control these sorts of unconscious urges better than dogs, we are still susceptible to unconscious patterns of behavior. An action that we found useful at a meaningful moment in our life can become engrained to a point where we are barely aware of our behavior. These habits can be benign (like absentmindedly driving to the old office where you worked for years, long after you started your new job across town) or harmful (being stuck in cycles of abusive relationships after learning relationship skills in an abusive childhood home). Even when habitual actions are repeatedly punished, their resilience in the face of reminiscent conditions can be profound.

But there's a silver lining. For any animal—including people and dogs—old habits may die hard, but creating new habits can be almost instantaneous in the right circumstances. You may solve some problems virtually overnight once you step back and look at the bigger picture. You may notice pieces of the puzzle that you hadn't considered, and open up possibilities for change. When you discover how to use other factors to your advantage—especially those in the environment—you've got a second chance at learning. Our ability to make new choices and learn new strategies is far more than just a matter of rewards and punishments. For humans, dogs, and everything in between, game-changing conditions can create game-changing opportunities for behavioral change.

## Awkward Impulses

So here you are, ready to embrace the window of opportunity provided by learning, excited to show your dog how to make better choices and build more practical habits for your life together. But we all know that we can't entirely escape the influence of our past. Before you start working on that list of dog behaviors you plan to change, you are going to need to start with a critical reality check. No matter how hard you try, how perfect the conditions inside and out, there are inherent limitations. You have to accept him for what he was born with—those habits far beyond his control. There are things he can't change. There are actions he may not be able to stop, and new habits he will be unable to acquire.

Why would your dog turn in multiple circles before he lies down, bedding and perfecting the imaginary grass that isn't there, on the living room rug? Why would he use his nose to bury his bone on the sofa with dirt that clearly isn't there? As you just learned, the answer is that it runs in the canine family.

These genetic, learned impulses are like potential energy just waiting for the cue from life to engage—a behavioral software program ready to run at the click of a mouse as some environmental trigger stimulates that primal lizard brain. A great many modern dog behavior "problems" arise when this happens for our pets. Out of their original context, these once-useful impulses can wreak havoc in our homes or have serious consequences for a dog's mental health if they are suppressed altogether. When a naturally meaningful sensory signal (i.e., a huntable animal) stirs a behavioral key for your dog (to hunt it) and he is unable to engage with a fitting outlet (always on a leash, nothing else to hunt), he becomes frustrated. If this happens repeatedly or chronically, your dog's behavior can become dysfunctional. The behavioral habit has nowhere to go.

If an impulse continues to fold in on itself in frustration, it can become neurotic in expression. That's right—dogs, just like people, can develop neuroses. And just like us, these kinds of dysfunctional behaviors are frequently the indicators that our genes have found themselves in the wrong place at the wrong time.

The collie who was bred to herd sheep, living in the condo without a flock, spins and barks. The pointer bred to visually freeze on game birds stares for hours at shadows on the wall. The terrier bred to tenaciously prey on small fast-moving animals chases its own tail in madness. The retriever bred to carry the game bird in his mouth develops an oral fixation with balls and his own front leg. Obsessive-compulsive behaviors like these can develop from an inherited habit, an instinctual impulse, genetically developed but unable to express itself appropriately. For modern pet dogs living in worlds very different from those for which their breed developed, this is a common problem. The imbalance between genetics and a modern environment creates friction and ripple effects for behavioral health.

You cannot educate a genetically learned instinct out of your dog. Period. So it is your job to recognize these kinds of genetic impulses present in your dog and direct them into appropriate and healthy outlets of expression in his environment whenever you can. And yet, while impulses are instinctual, they are also flexible. Those outlets do not have to fit the historical purpose of the behavior to a T, as long as they are sufficiently satisfying to the animal by being close enough to the natural behavior that they can stimulate the impulse, arouse the dog's system into an alternative appropriate action, and offer that rushing reinforcement of dopamine. Sanity—for him, and therefore for you—can arise from your creativity as you work to find ways to let your dog be who he was born to be in a healthy way.

You don't have to buy a flock of sheep or let your terrier go on a rat-killing rampage. You can build intense daily routines of exercise that work in your world—whether it's ball-herding through the house or plush-toy-murdering in the yard. You can take the edge off of his frustration and neuroticism by offering these alternatives to less-palatable behaviors that threaten other animals and people. Still, you do need to accept that these behavioral keys without their original environmental locks can present enormous challenges for him, and for you. You can successfully manage your companion's interactions with the world around him so that those instinctual habits that run in the family don't get him in big trouble. But be realistic enough to unburden yourself of the expectation that he should be capable of obedience to you in the face of these powerful impulses; realize what you both are up against when it comes to learning that runs so deep.

## Learned Habits

So what about habits that aren't inherited from grandparents? Behaviors that we pick up in our own lives are surely deliberate and controllable, right? If we learned something, we should be able to unlearn it. And so should the dog. Unfortunately, once a habit has been formed, it's not quite that simple.

Your alarm goes off at 6 a.m. You mindlessly stumble into the shower and begin the morning routine you repeat every single day. You open the door of your car with your left hand, holding your coffee in your right hand, and climb in to drive the same route to work. You arrive and park in the same place and walk into the same door to set that coffee mug in the same place on the same desk before beginning yet another day on the job. You meet the inevitable curveballs of lost homework, spilled orange juice, and flat tires as they arise along the way, but you repeat most of these daily actions automatically without any thought at all.

The complex sequences of movements required for such mundane things as brushing your teeth or driving your car have been successfully repeated so many times that they occur almost effortlessly. Like well-worn riverbeds, the neural pathways underlying these actions now flow with ease. Behaviors once new and overwhelming to you (the first time driving a stick shift, using your new coffeepot, or making a spreadsheet) have become so routine that they virtually repeat themselves. They are habits.

Anyone who has ever tried to change a habit knows how hard it can be. The new girlfriend moves in and wants you to stop leaving your toothbrush on the bathroom sink, perpetually annoyed to find it in the same place months after she admonished you for failing to put it away. It's not that you don't care. You just don't even really notice where you're putting it anymore. You have been brushing your teeth in that bathroom for five years, putting your toothbrush down in the exact same place every day. You aren't trying to be disrespectful or cause problems in the relationship. But she takes this toothbrush business pretty personally.

Similar events happen in your relationship with your dog. Some of your dog's behavior works out pretty well for her and is repeated, becoming a habit over time that could ultimately drive you crazy. For no reason you can identify, she has broken out of her crate every day since you adopted her, chewing up at least one valuable item (remote control, your diary, a pair of new shoes) each time you leave home. She barks and jumps frantically whenever you walk through the door. She has eaten eight pairs of underwear this month and chased at least one hot guy out of your life. She ignores your yelling and pleading amid tears of exasperation. It feels personal. She has been with you for six months now, so she should relax and trust that you will come home. Why won't she learn?

She *has* learned. She has learned well. In fact, she's got escaping from a crate down to a science—because she was left for excessive periods of time in a crate at her last home, and she perfected her skills. In her previous home, chewing things up apparently continued to bring people back; and it relieved a great deal of frustration after ten hours of confinement in a box. Jumping all over the humans upon their return gets a response: the undivided attention she'd been craving for hours in their absence. Just because she is in a healthy home with you now—crated only for short periods of time, exercised extensively, spoiled with chew toys, and indulged with attention—does not mean that these habitual responses to being left alone will simply vanish.

# Replacing the Ritual

**THE SITUATION:** Your dog goes crazy, jumping and shrieking, at the front door every time you have guests over.

**WHAT YOU DO:** Keep your dog behind a baby gate when guests first enter your house and give your dog a long-lasting, exclusive "visitor bone". Eating scrumptious butcher bones can totally redefine the meaning of company and may finally break the cycle of craziness at the front door. After several times of experiencing this, your dog will begin to associate visitors with the anticipation of receiving a yummy goody.

**WHY IT WORKS:** Through your actions, you dam the old habitual mode of behavior with the baby gate and encourage a new mindset with the golden chewy, and voilà—you have a new behavioral path for your dog to take when a friend comes knocking. Eventually, he will run into the kitchen and wait for the super "visitor bone".

Long after she relaxes into her life with you and her anxiety falls away, she still breaks out to find a chosen object to chew while awaiting your dramatic return. These behaviors have become habitual to her; sequences of behaviors chained together, they arise in a given scenario—watching through the bars of the crate as a person walks out the front door. These behaviors are now a part of her routine. They may not be intentional, or even conscious.

It's important to recognize when our dog's past experience has set the stage for those very resilient habits we observe and wish to change. Becoming unduly offended or personalizing the actions of our canine friend creates resentment, false judgment, and even premature hopelessness about the relationship. Many habits can and will change with the right approach; new neural pathways can be carved out and the old ones effectively dammed.

If we are understanding about the power of habits, we may patiently cultivate new substitute habits, gradually rendering the old ones meaningless. We can be realistic about the amount of time it takes to carve out a new course of action in a mind where the old course has been well traveled for so long. We can be creative about the introduction of new game-changing learning that is spontaneous and powerful, shifting other factors in critical ways for the benefit of the relationship.

## Individual Choices—Opening New Doors of Learning

All too often, we pull our hair out as we continue to do the same thing over and over ("No! Sit! Stay!"), getting the same maddening results. We totally miss the leverage right under our nose—our ability to control the environment for our dog in order to invite new choices.

*What happens when I . . . ? I wonder if I could . . . ? How can I . . . ?* These are the kinds of inspiring questions behind the choices we make when life hands us a new set of conditions. Our brain probably won't even bother to ask these questions if we have a precedent to go on. Whatever action we have done the last few times (or thousands of times) in a similar moment will just kick in if we have already learned a habit or impulse that had a desirable consequence. We ask these questions only when something is different or new, or when a previous strategy is no longer working for us.

Before you get your dog to ask the important *How can I . . . ?* question that can pave the way for new choices in behavior (rather than continuing to just do what has worked for her in the past), you have to ask that question of yourself. You need to change the big picture in order to break your half of the cycle. If she can continue to get what she desires by behaving in a way you find undesirable, she has no reason whatsoever to ask herself how she could do things differently. But if she finds herself in a suddenly different scenario, one in which her old stand-by behavior won't work anymore, she will become curious and creative about a possible plan B. Think about what your goal is, what you are trying to accomplish, and what role you have to play in setting your dog up for success.

Like so many things in life, making new choices is about instilling a fresh perspective in order to get us out of a rut. Nature has wired both you and your dog so that, when conditions are new, you give life your undivided attention; and you become creative and experimental in your actions. Looked at from a different vantage point, the world is suddenly filled with possibilities.

Understanding how *impulses* and *habits* are formed, and how new *choices* are made, is all about recognizing the role of all four L.E.G.S.® in the process. Patterns of behavior can become very damaging until we know how to break them; so it is in the interest of both you and your dog to have a good relationship. If you're ever feeling stuck or at your wits' end with your dog, remember to stop and think about the problem objectively. Analyze the pieces of the puzzle that contribute to the unwanted cycles. When the L.E.G.S.® are aligned in new ways, you may be surprised at how easy it can be to make changes for both of you.

# Dinnertime Do-Over: A Winning Strategy for Learning with L.E.G.S.®

Your dog hounds you during mealtimes. She whines and barks, scratches your leg, and occasionally licks the table. It's obnoxious and gross. Years of yelling haven't deterred her. There are four elements you can make adjustments to in order to capture your dog's attention and create new *choices* and *habits*.

## ♥ What you need:

A chew-proof tether or a leash. Clip or tie one end to the foot of a heavy piece of furniture leg such as your couch, or an eye hook secured to a baseboard; or use a doorstop tether (a chew-proof short leash with a stopper on one end so you can slide it under any door for a convenient and movable restraint system).

## ♥ What you do:

Leash her to the foot of the couch/hook/door, away from the dinner table (but in the same room) whenever you serve food.

## ♥ Why this will change her behavior:

**YOU ARE CHANGING THE ENVIRON-MENT.** Novelty creates opportunity and attention. In the traditional language of learning, they call the environmental stage the *antecedent* (A). It is the condition that triggers a *behavior* (B) in order to affect a *consequence* (C). Your dog has already figured out the ABC's of a behavior (in this case, begging), and a certain stage is set (dinner is served at the table with her at your side). In this situation, if you expect her to stop the behavior, you are swimming against the tide of history. But reintroduce the situation with a new condition (she is leashed to the foot of the couch across the room with a bone before you serve the meal), and you've gotten your dog's attention. This prevents her from engaging the old habit automatically, and gives you the chance to answer the *How can I . . . ?* question (in this case, *How can I . . . get your dinner?*) that she is suddenly asking again.

**YOU ARE MANAGING THE LEARNED HABIT.** If a behavior continues to work out well for your dog, she will continue to do it. Life might be reinforcing her for continuing to beg (people do drop yummy things regularly, especially when kids are involved), and her brain is chemically rewarding her for trying even when she fails. It is an impossible cycle to break unless you manage it (your dog is leashed to that couch whenever food is served) to prevent it beginning at all. Be diligent about preventing your dog from begging around meals by using leashes, doors, baby gates, crates, etc., until you have adjusted the behavior.

**YOU ARE EXPLOITING THE GENETIC MOTIVATION.** You will never persuade your little scavenger to lose interest in table scraps, but you can put her love of them to work for you. It is in her DNA to seek leftovers from human meals. Once you have played the first two cards, you can win the hand by putting the force of this genetic impulse to work for you rather than against you. At the end of your meal, put some leftovers or other goodies in her bowl *only* if she remained quiet while you ate.

**YOU ARE MINDING THE SELF.** A young puppy has far less impulse control, attention span, and maturity than an older dog. However, she also is behaviorally far more creative and experimental, without the baggage of habits in her way. An older dog may have maturity, but also has had plenty of time to practice bad habits. If your dog was recently rescued from conditions in which she was starved, it may take her longer to learn to control herself around food than if she were fat and happy.

**THE RESULT:** Your dog can't reach the table scraps anymore, can't practice begging, can't hunt for scraps under the table during dinnertime, and can't get reinforced for the behavior that disrupts the family meals. She might make some noise on the leash the first few times you do this, until she discovers that it's useless to do so. If she's noisy, she is invisible to you over there on that leash. She has to get creative and experimental because the old jig is up, and her drama isn't working. You now have her attention (the conditions are new because she is leashed to the couch and can't reach the table) and new choices are possible (the old begging strategy can't work from across the room). You have set up a new ABC. You aren't fighting the impulse to scavenge and beg anymore. Instead, you are exploiting it—showing her *how* to get in on dinnertime now that her old ways are failing.

You have created a new situation in which she gets to clean up under the table *after* dinner if she remained quiet and relaxed on her leash throughout the meal. If she complains about it, she will remain on the leash until she decides to try being quiet, and you will have cleaned up all the scraps before you let her loose to sniff around. You will be surprised how quickly she gets on board. After a few meals, you probably won't even need the leash anymore. She can try being loose and experiment with her choices again. Maybe if she lies quietly on the rug just a few feet away,

you will let her remain closer to the table and off of the leash? Yes. Okay, dog. That's fine. Maybe she will try coming up to you and whining just a teeny weeny bit? No; not so much, dog. Back to the leash you go for the rest of dinner.

You will let her find out that hovering or pushing or vocalizing around the table gets her leashed to the couch and results in no scrap-finding after dinner. You will let her discover that staying by the couch or lying somewhere quietly for the duration of the meal results in scrap enjoyment afterward (maybe even some of those meaty plate scrapings in her bowl). You have showed her a new way to scavenge effectively, one that works even better than the last. And in the process, you have taught her to be polite during meals in under a week's time.

## Life Lessons

Every moment in life is potentially a memorable one. We never know how an experience will affect our perceptions, attitudes, ideas, behaviors, and habits. Life is constantly reshaping us. People, pets, places, and things become meaningful to us; and those meanings change over time. We learn how to do new things and develop behaviors and routines in our lives according to the changing circumstances around us, and we acquire occasional baggage along the way. We learn naturally, because nature has designed each of us animals to notice, experiment, discover, and remember in order to survive.

Dogs are no exception. They are having their own experiences, trying to figure it all out as they go, just like you. They are trying to make sense of the world around them, and trying to navigate through it as well as they can in order to be successful. You are an important part of that world—quite possibly the most important of all.

Relationships play profound roles in our lives as social creatures, and the "pet" arrangement puts an even greater emphasis on the relationship between you and your dog. In many ways, your lives can't help but revolve around each other as you continue to experience and learn. You are inescapably meaningful to each other, and inextricably involved in each other's daily habits and routines. Neither one is ever quite independent of the other. This makes for a pretty intense relationship at times. It also creates a precious chance to experience life intimately with another being.

Life will have many lessons for you both. Sometimes those lessons are not easy. Not all partners and conditions are ultimately compatible, and some aspects of the L.E.G.S.® are just beyond our control. While there are inevitable hard knocks in the pursuit of a happy relationship, we can commit to setting the stage for positive change when the going gets tough. There are plenty of things we *can* change. You can make the love between you and your dog new again as you put the pieces together with a fresh perspective. You can set the stage for new learning for both of you by changing conditions to create new habits that will transform the relationship.

# CHAPTER THREE

# Environment

When you walk into the office dressed in a three-piece suit, ready for an arraignment at the courthouse, you are the epitome of the career-driven professional. The interns are a little scared of you, as you strut down the hall in your heels, knowing you've got that high-profile case totally in the bag. Later that night, however, when you're at home watching old reruns of *The Golden Girls* in your shark pajamas and eating a bowl of ice cream for dinner, you appear to be someone else entirely.

You may act super goofy and lighthearted around your best friend, but you're quiet at big parties and kind of a grumpy micromanager when your brother's kids come over and ransack your personal space. You can be blue-jeans tomboy or elegant lady dressed to kill or sentimental '80s sitcom fan, depending on the context. You wear many hats, changing them to adapt to the occasion and to your environment.

You might not imagine that your little buddy—drooling on the couch over your bowl of ice cream—can relate, but he most definitely can. His actions, just like yours, are highly contextual. Moment to moment, your behavior changes (often unconsciously) in response to the world and conditions around you. Your environment is constantly prompting you to respond to various demands. You are a chameleon in an ever-changing landscape because you have to be—and so is he. You have both learned to change in order to fit in, get along, and be successful. Neither of you is immune to the world around you. In fact, the world has *a lot* to do with how you behave. It should be pretty obvious that no one is an island. But sometimes we forget that.

A relationship may shatter when one partner—who fell in love with the attractive and apparently organized coworker previously seen only in boardrooms and fancy restaurants—turns out to be a total slob in his own home. Seeing how your boyfriend behaves at a bar, in contrast to cross-examining a witness in court, can be eye-opening. Similarly, it may be horrifying to watch your sweet beagle kill a baby rabbit when you take him to visit your uncle's farm. It's confusing, too; you know him only as the gentle dog who snuggles with cats. When we suddenly encounter a side of our companion (person or animal) that we haven't seen before, we may lament and panic. We make accusations and jump to conclusions. We say things like, "You're *different*. You've *changed*. You're not who I thought you were." Somehow we expect the people and pets around us to be static and predictable in all situations, even though we ourselves are not. We forget to consider the environmental circumstances behind others' changes in behavior.

We fall into this trap with our dogs all the time. A dog owner finds herself considering a new home for her beloved retriever after she witnessed him snapping at a toddler; she's convinced he is finally revealing his natural aggression, or else is dangerously possessed. "I don't understand. He *loves* kids. He has always been friendly to them. I don't understand why he has *changed* all of a sudden." What the owner hasn't considered is that the two of them just moved into her boyfriend's house, where five-year-old twin boys and a two-year-old with no concept of personal space treat the dog like living-room furniture. The dog didn't change—the *environment* did. The dog's behavior is only a response to a new loud and scary land.

The environment influences our dog's actions at any given time. When we have questions or concerns, we need to give due consideration to this powerful catalyst for behavior. Before we say to our dog, "What in the world were you thinking?" we would be wise to ask ourselves *what in the world* might be causing his behavior. Remember to examine the role of the environment for the incredible opportunities in addition to the serious obstacles it can present. The devil is often in the details; and those environmental details can make or break the relationship with your dog.

## The Right Shoes

The value of this cannot be overstated: Simply pause to consider the circumstances your dog is in. We expect uniform reliability, no matter what the moment brings. We sure don't mean to, but we forget to take a look around and do the math. Maybe it's not the thing, the partner, or the dog that is failing. It's quite possible that they're having a hard time fitting in with the environment.

After all, those stilettos just won't do in the gym. And you might lose your job if you wore your shark pajamas to the hearing. The environment you're in, at any given moment, has a lot to do with your behaviors (and how things play out as a result).

Apply this logic to your expectations and practices in your relationship with your dog. Examine the circumstances around you and your dog constantly, and help him with those environmental shoes to make sure that they fit. Your ability to manipulate the environment to his benefit may be greater than you think. Don't stack the deck against your dog—and yourself—by leaving the environmental stone unturned.

Small changes can yield fast results and can eradicate problems almost overnight. You fence in the yard; and suddenly your dog spends half his day enjoying the great outdoors instead of eating the sheetrock. You triple his exercise; and he's no longer pacing and whining when you watch TV for more than an hour. You make a new rule that the kids are no longer allowed to play near his food bowl—and he hasn't growled at them since. A simple request you made to your landlord, that he come by for repairs only when you are home, has stopped his complaints about your dog's incessant barking while he fixes the pipes. All sorts of problems—boredom, anxiety, icky habits, and potential disasters—may be resolved with the right changes to your dog's environment.

When you *cannot* adjust the necessary details of life, the environment may present deal-breaking conditions to which you or your dog will sometimes simply be unable to adapt. Nature has its limitations, and the environment often reveals them. The workaholic farm-bred sheepdog can't just flip a switch and become a mellow couch potato confined to a studio apartment in Manhattan for twenty-two hours a day—any more than you can suddenly become a laid-back supernanny to a houseful of visiting nephews leaping from your new furniture in a reenacted light-saber duel from *Star Wars*. In both cases, you might as well try to make your home at the bottom of the ocean. You cannot become something you are not; and certain circumstances simply are incompatible with your nature and needs. Anyone can become anxious or aggressive, problematic or neurotic, or utterly dysfunctional when the fundamental key to who they are doesn't fit the lock of the world around them.

An environment—a habitat—is more than a backdrop to life. It is a complicated ecosystem of conditions, signals, events, and interactions that work with the physical and behavioral shape of the animal or against it. There is a niche for every creature—a part made just for them in the play of life—in which they feel at home and function productively for themselves as well as the other species in that system.

A dog's niche and natural place has consistently been by mankind's side as a professional human behavior observer, manipulator, and opportunist. Dogs stick around us because it pays well to do so. They acquired leftovers from people (the stuff we didn't want after a hunt or meal), and developed a variety of genius adaptive gestures (look cute, raise your paw, whimper a little, wag your tail). They also developed skills (linger around places people eat and move in quickly for dropped food bits, raid garbage dumps for goodies) in and around our respective villages. In return, humans have received help securing and protecting resources. Whether it was a dog who could passionately track the scent of our game over harsh terrain, one who would reliably help us to move livestock from one pasture to another with organized precision, or a scrappy hunter intent on ridding our settlements of troublesome rodents—dogs were molded into experts in remarkably different niches. They were distinctly customized from one another to fit a range of specialized roles within our human lives.

The environments we inhabit with our dogs have changed rapidly (unprecedentedly so) in the last century. Few of us are shepherds, hunters, or farmers anymore. Most of the dogs' jobs have been taken by technology or are no longer needed. The modern industrialized environments we offer our dogs today are not always a good fit for our canine companions. We need to be able to understand how these tensions are created in the modern lifestyles we share with our dogs so that we can soften the problematic edges.

As you learn about the vital elements of your dog's lifestyle in this chapter—their "work life," "home life," "public life," "personal life," "family life," etc.—keep asking yourself if the environment that you are providing or creating for your dog actually fits your dog. You may find that, with a little insight, creative flexibility, good planning, and commitment to compromise, you can make some necessary adjustments. You can see your shared world through your dog's eyes, and appreciate how important those many external circumstances are to the health of your dog and to your relationship.

## On the Job

It's the perfect job for you. After years of dreading the sound of the alarm clock in the morning as you faced another day as a corporate executive, you now spring out of bed with excitement. Why? Because you love your new job at the hospital. It sounds a little hokey, but you really feel like you have found your calling as a nurse's assistant. The emptiness and frustration that defined your reality for so long seems like a distant memory now. You barely recognize the person you were then.

You took to this new job like you were born for it—calculating doses and inserting IVs in the ER with the grace and speed of a ninja your very first week. Who would have thought that ten-hour shifts surrounded by human secretions and high-stress emergencies would be good for your chronic anxiety? This job is the perfect fit for you; it just clicks. Your world has completely changed, and so have you.

It may be hard to fathom that our dogs could have such a similar life experience. While they may not contemplate a change in their daily "jobs" exactly the way we do, a dog may be even more negatively affected by an ill-fitting position than we are. As with any specialist who becomes increasingly customized for a particular niche, dogs have developed into occupational experts who thrive in their element and struggle outside of it. Most of the dogs we know today were bred into specific professions as herders, guardians, wrestlers, hunters, and trackers. The knowledge of the job—what it looks like, feels like, smells like, and sounds like, and what to do about it—is in their bones.

The environmental details of those various occupations—long days alongside shepherds moving flocks of sheep over harsh mountain ranges to greener pastures, or long nights as castle watchmen patiently patrolling vast perimeters and lying in wait for formidable invaders—defined the very shape and character of the dogs we humans would develop throughout history. Whether it was locating the scent of a specific game bird among the reeds and thickets, sparring for a roaring crowd, or hunting down varmint thieves in their dark holes and slaying them, the job became ever more important for our dogs as we continued to specialize their genetic templates to our advantage. These workers were in their element when they recognized the signals in the world around them and knew exactly what to do. Like a highly specialized tool, carefully selected for the specific demands of the job, these animals fit perfectly the environmental task at hand.

As animals were bred for a certain behavior, for a valuable performance in one set of conditions, the very nature of dogs was also changed in important ways. Some got lighter on their feet and some got heavier. Some became bolder and more independent, while others became more passive and dependent on humans. Some got quieter and some got louder. Some hunted animals; others protected them. Some bit gently, some bit severely, and some refrained from biting altogether. Some grew more responsive to us while others became impervious to interruptions. Some lived in the field alongside the flock, while others stayed at our bedside. All of these differences occurred as a direct result of our impressive ability to re-create our dogs according to the job and the environment.

While these genetic changes made our dogs better suited to specific environments and demands, they made them less flexible and adaptive to *other* kinds of circumstances. For example, though the collie's hypervigilance and quick response to sudden movements enabled us to move a flock to an exact location with great precision and efficiency, such behavior was not only useless but infuriating outside of this context. The more specific the job, the more specific the animals' needs in their environment became; and, as a result, they often became poorly suited to anything else.

In a modern world where so many of those jobs no longer exist, these dogs often find themselves in the same position of boredom, frustration, and misery that we do when we're at our wits' end in the wrong job. You can appreciate how challenging it might be—given the circumstances of his chronic dissatisfaction with his employment (or lack thereof)—for your animal to just relax, chew his bone by the fire, and be a "good" dog. He might feel like an overqualified expert in a completely dead job market in his field.

You will soon be able to satisfy your dog's need for purpose—for the right occupation—as you write him a meaningful new job description well suited to his professional background, skills, abilities, and interests. You may not be able to provide him with a field of rabbits or a flock of sheep, but you can take him into the woods to track animal scents or teach him to herd soccer balls at the field behind the high school. Your hands aren't as tied as they might seem. You can fill his cup and ease his mind. Chances are, if you do, you will see results immediately.

## In the Home

You just walked through the door after a long, exhausting day at the hospital. Your dog is barking frantically in his crate in the bedroom. You put down the groceries, pick up the leash, and open the bedroom door in horror as you observe the shreds of your new comforter all over the floor around his crate. The expensive bedspread you saved for months to buy was attractive to him, too—and within his reach. Furious, you open the latch and admonish him for his destruction in your absence, knowing you will now be rushed to clean up this mess in time for your dinner party tonight. *Why on earth would he chew up that blanket when he had a crate full of toys to play with, not to mention his own darn bed to destroy?* The family you got him from said he'd never chewed up anything of theirs before; but then again they also had a fenced-in yard with two other dogs. And they worked from home. Could that really make such a difference?

You take him out for a quick pee. After spending ten minutes looking for the perfect place to take a leak, he does his business and reluctantly follows you back into the apartment. You rush to change your clothes and begin cooking dinner. He follows you from room to room, inches behind you at every step, whining and jumping at your dress. You feed him, hoping to occupy his attention for a moment and satisfy his extreme neediness.

The doorbell rings thirty minutes too soon when your first friend arrives for dinner. Your dog eagerly greets her with barking and jumping on *her* dress. You give him a bone and tell him to go lie down. He does. For about thirty seconds. Then he is back up, scrambling for attention from both of you as you try to catch your friend up on the latest news. But you can't even hear yourself think (much less hear your friend talk) over his whining and barking. Three more friends arrive, and the same thing happens with each guest, so you put him in the bedroom. You spend the next twenty minutes imagining your bedspread being torn into even more pieces behind the door, so you decide to bring him back into the dining room with a new toy when you all sit down for dinner. He behaves—relatively—throughout the meal, and you give him a leftover piece of food as you put him back into the crate (away from the bed this time) before going out for the evening with your friends.

*He spent twelve hours in the crate today,* you think to yourself guiltily as you fall asleep with him that night. *I wonder if that's too long. Maybe he's bored. Maybe he's lonely.* "I'm sorry, buddy," you tell him as you kiss him. "I'll get up early in the morning and we'll go on a long walk before I go to work. Surely the extra hour out of the house will make you feel better. I'll bring you home a new bone from the shop too, okay?" He kisses you back and you feel a little better. You really love this dog, and you want to figure out how to make it work.

As you leave the next day for the hospital, you set your sights on your patients as he sets his on another eight hours alone in a crate and another twenty-three hours of his day spent indoors (well, twenty-two given the longer walk that morning and the one you plan on after work). You drive home that evening, preparing for your longer-than-usual walk with him before returning emails, calling your mom, and catching your favorite show before bed. He will follow you adorably from room to room as usual, wide-eyed and panting, and relentlessly bring you that stupid squeaky ball to throw whenever you sit down. This pet thing isn't quite as easy as you thought it would be—for either of you.

## The Modern "Pet" Environment

Imagine being involuntarily stuck on an airplane for an eight-hour flight every day only to land, greet your family, walk around the airport, use the restroom, and step outside for a few moments of fresh air—before returning to the terminal and waiting to board the plane again alone in the morning. It would get old really fast. Just imagine what it must be like for your dog, if he is anything like the average "pet" dog, to have such limited space, limited movement, and limited access to the outdoors on a daily basis. That life, even if pleasant enough, can become maddeningly unfulfilling, repetitive, and frustrating.

Your dog's only apparent option is to find ways to get *any* interesting game going to pass the time—breaking into the garbage, chewing the table, stealing your socks, chasing the kitty, barking at the TV, whining at you while you're on the phone. We call that misbehavior. But, for many of our pet dogs, this is life. And sometimes they are losing their ever-loving minds over it.

With all of the realistic demands of modern life you are facing and only so many hours in a day to meet them, there is only so much you can do. And there is only so much *he* can do. The reality is that a pet environment—for most dogs, regardless of what they were bred to do—is almost entirely indoors and highly inactive. It can cause sensory overload due to the lack of emotional and physical outlets for the dog, even as it is simultaneously impossibly boring for him. Without a way to take any action or control his environment, his senses can feel ready to burst. Think eight-hour delay in a crowded international airport and you'll have the idea.

While you are living a busy life, it can easily escape your attention that your beloved dog might be struggling. You make every effort to meet his needs, but you have to go to work and pay the bills. You need to go to the store and the post office, have to return those phone calls and emails. You really are doing everything you know to do as a pet owner, giving him everything you possibly can while still making a living and having a life.

But this kind of domestic life is taking a toll on him. He doesn't have the option of doing something else, of getting his own life or hobbies. He can't just decide to get off the plane and walk out of the airport to other horizons. He relies on you, his doting keeper, for absolutely everything in his life. You are responsible for his meals, his health, his entertainment, his social life, his exercise, and ultimately his sanity.

Don't let this discourage you. Your unique position also gives you the ability to change your dog's world for the better. You may not be able to quit your job, but you can find a thousand ways to enrich his in order to get him off of unemployment. You can get him outside as much as possible, and take him to places off the beaten path. You can shamelessly chase squirrels up trees with him or take him swimming in the ocean. You can help him make new meaningful friends and foster his own relationships. You can give your creative genius hard puzzles to solve in order to earn his breakfast rather than serve him another easy plate of food and watch him unravel the mysteries of your bathrobe. You can ask him to be your wingman, teach him how the modern world requires that he behave in order to accompany you on your many snazzy adventures. You can take him out for dinner and a night on the town after a run through the park and the perfect sweet sunset on the hill in the summer air.

Realizing how much your dog leans on you to open the doors to a greater world for him, you can start to open them one by one. Meeting his environmental needs on a daily basis—once you recognize them—will improve life immeasurably both for you and for him.

Sometimes your hands are tied in terms of what you can change about your dog's home life. But compassion for his predicament can reduce your frustration and resentment. You'll see that the bedspread destruction (and the incessant party-crashing barking, whining, and jumping) wasn't personal at all. You may be inspired to take steps to expand his horizons beyond the walls of your house and to create a better home life for both of you.

Your dog needs to get out and live it up a little. He needs you to provide those chances for him to do whatever his heart desires in a safe environment. You are, after all, not the only one who gets cabin fever and needs a change of scenery, and the chance to let your hair down after hours of confinement indoors. He, too, hungers desperately for the right career path and those occasional chances to really blow off some steam. And, like you, he just isn't quite right without these things.

## In the Neighborhood

So, out you go—into the world, confident and ambitious about putting some real meaning and purpose into his life as you clip on the leash and step out the door after a long day at work. You exchange a heartfelt glance with him as you ride the elevator down to the first floor. The way he's looking at you makes you think he can read your mind, that he is touched by your newly inspired commitment to provide the adventure he so desperately needs. You can't wait to walk down the street, head to the park for a run, and stop by the coffee shop on the way home to meet friends. This is going to be incredible for both of you. You just know it.

Until your peaceful moment is suddenly shattered by looming potential disaster ahead. You see a woman approaching you with a couple of large dogs enthusiastically straining like sled dogs in your direction. It seems improbable that the one-hundred-pound woman walking them has any control of them whatsoever, and you hold your breath as she yells out, "They're friendly!" and surges toward you, behind her team of wide-eyed, smiling Labradors. Your dog starts to growl as they break an invisible fifty-yard line, and then escalates into a fit of high-pitched wails and barks as they close in. The labs might be friendly, all right, but they're sure coming on pretty strong to a couple of total strangers.

The woman makes no apparent attempt to stop them from ambushing your dog as she goes by, calling them "silly boys" as she drags them onward down the street as your little buddy hides behind your legs and snaps at them. You're torn between anger and shame as you make your final turn toward the park. Your dog *did* look like a rabid little beaver there for a minute, gnashing his teeth at them. Are those his true colors showing? Did he *change* from the cool and confident dog you were walking with just moments before? You shake your head and come to your senses. How would you feel in that situation? Given the circumstances, is there really something *wrong* with the way your dog was acting?

The truth is, most of us have unrealistic expectations for our dogs' behavior—far beyond what we would ever expect from any other animal, person, or child. It's pure fantasy that dogs will be the uniformly friendly, social, outgoing, bombproof, affectionate, tolerant, unopinionated, and complacent creatures we want them to be out in the world. This Lab-wielding woman is just one of many naïve and innocent dog owners effectively conditioned to the mindset that expects all "good" dogs to like everybody and everything regardless of the circumstance.

# Don't Pop My Bubble!

You know how you feel when someone invades your personal space inappropriately, how the hair stands up on the back of your neck and you suddenly are a little defensive or want to get away? Even when you logically know that person is not a threat, it makes you uncomfortable if they approach you abruptly, stand a little too close when you're talking, or touch you without invitation. It's because you, like all animals, have something called *flight distance*—the space it would take for you to feel out of harm's way in case you needed to get away suddenly. It's the imaginary bubble around you that creates your comfort zone of personal space, and you get very prickly when it's popped.

For you, this natural personal space bubble is somewhere in the neighborhood of a foot or two (depending on your culture and heritage). For a highly domesticated species like the modern human, natural flight distance has been reduced over time as populations have increased and people have had to live in closer proximity (think big cities). So we can stand being pretty darn close to each other without getting uncomfortable, particularly if we are minding our own business (such as on a subway or in line). We just assume our dog's sense of personal space is the same as ours. But it is not.

Most dogs have a flight distance of somewhere between seven and ten feet. Yes, that means that another person or dog is officially in your dog's personal space bubble when they cross that invisible line. For dogs who are genetically domesticated to pet conditions, it can be a little less. But many dogs maintain this greater sense of personal space, and react strongly when it is invaded by other people and animals. We usually blame these dogs for acting out, unaware that their bubble has been popped.

Once you know about the bubble, you can navigate the neighborhood and greater world with your dog and avoid a thousand accidents simply by protecting that space. When you walk down the street, imagine a seven-foot bubble around you and your dog as you move along, and distance yourself from others in order to prevent them from popping it. If you don't have enough room or time to create the distance, put yourself between your dog and the figurative needle.

Like the one-car-length rule many drivers practice to avoid rear-end collisions, this practice can help prevent a thousand uncomfortable moments for you and your dog. Understanding how his flight distance works will also help you appreciate how often your dog feels backed into a corner. So much of the time, when we might think his behavior is unwarranted, bizarre, or unprovoked, he is just naturally responding to the uncomfortable situations that we and others accidentally put him in. It's your job to keep his bubble from getting popped, so keep your eyes on the road and be a defensive driver!

When you take your dog out into the world, you will be inundated by a host of well-intentioned fellow dog lovers who let their "friendly" dogs, children, and spouses pop the bubble of your dog's personal space. Your dog will be expected not only to tolerate it, but to like it and to participate merrily in these interactions. Dogs who do not happen to fit the mold of these social pet customs we have adopted, and who protest in any way (barking, snarling, snapping, hiding) will be labeled as "bad" or in need of training or "fixing." They are expected to learn how to let it all roll off of them whether they like it or not.

Some kinds of dogs will handle these expectations better than others. Some have been selectively bred for social complacency and merriment.

But most have not. The majority of dogs in the population maintain the natural awareness of and concern for personal space and property, regard for the etiquette of introductions, and the value of minding one's own business. Others have been bred for suspicion and caution toward strange people and animals. Your dog should be allowed, as any member of our community should, to have his own personal space respected by other people and dogs when he goes out with his family. You shouldn't lose any sleep because that tenant accosted your dog and got growled at for it, after you asked her not to pet him. And you shouldn't buy into the label "aggressive" that the vet gave him, just because he was cornered and frightened by a strange dog in his least favorite establishment as he anxiously awaited his exam.

What you should do, however, is recognize how desperately he needs you to navigate the terrain of these obstacles and expectations for him. He needs you to recognize the fact that he is far from impervious to the conditions of this modern world. Just because he is affectionate with you and your mom's little Dachshund doesn't mean there is anything wrong with him for not wanting to cuddle a group of old ladies or play with the Boxer puppy at the park.

You can give him and yourself permission to not "say hi." You can rein him in and walk away when you see obnoxiously friendly dogs and people approaching, stand between him and the invasive two- and four-legged animals, and protect him from their reach. You can teach him how to take a back seat (figuratively "hold his hand" by keeping him close to you) and let you make the decisions about these things; teach him to trust you to handle life. You can show him how to behave on the street, at the café, and in the park in order to keep everybody happy and relaxed. You can have his back at all times. There is no need for you to feel guilty about protecting him from those uncomfortable, awkward, and stressful moments by keeping him close by under your wing as you cross paths with others on your adventures. He has every right to get out of the house and be a dog without fear of constant, albeit unintentional, harassment.

And if you happen to have one of those insanely outgoing, friendly, gregarious dogs who just wants to be everybody's best friend and has never met a stranger, that's great, too. But please know that your dog is actually the exception to the rule. His friendliness on the leash can be read by other dogs as threatening, even if he's only straining at the end of the leash in his great enthusiasm to make a new friend. You can do all your neighborhood dogs and owners a big favor and make sure to ask first before you let your dog introduce himself. Being a conscientious citizen about the natural, and perfectly acceptable, differences between dogs will mean more than you can possibly imagine to your fellow dog walkers on the road. For they *all* need—and deserve—to have an active life they can enjoy in peace.

You are determined to fill his cup in life with everything you've got. You are going to take him to that new dog adventure park you heard about so he can try his hand at tracking in the woods and swimming in the lake. Those hiking shoes and that trail map are coming out of the closet again. You want to help him find his natural calling and satisfy his instincts. But you also know that, most of your days, the best you will be able to do is take him along in the neighborhood and do what you can to let him live it up. You may not always be able to get him back into his element in the fields and forests from which he came, but you sure can appreciate and try to accommodate the culture shock he's very likely having every time he walks down the street in your twenty-first-century town. He can get used to it all, and even learn to relax and enjoy it all with you. But he needs your constant understanding, guidance, and protection in order to do so.

## In the Family

As fundamentally social animals, whoever we end up sharing our lives and homes with become critical elements of our overall environment. Inside of any family, the members are stuck in the same boat whether they like it or not. Whether it's a family of two or twelve, these fellow passengers instinctively sense that they are dependent on each other in some quintessential way. Some of our dogs needed to live in big social groups in order to hunt larger game and protect territories successfully, while others made a better living by breaking off into smaller and far less structured alliances in order to scavenge dispersed food sources such as garbage—not exactly requiring the benefits of larger numbers for a takedown of big game.

In the last century, dogs have increasingly found themselves in an entirely new kind of social environment, one barely resembling those of their ancestral past. As our "pets," dogs are in fixed, captive, mixed-species social groups comprised of whatever people and pets we allow to share our home. These are not packs. Nor is this the life of the free-roaming village dogs found all over the world.

All in all, our dogs are pretty darn amenable to what we have thrown at them. They don't speak the same language as most of their shipmates, and have entirely different customs and habits. Most of them have lost all of their independence, their freedom, their careers, and their autonomous ability to pursue their own interests. Nonetheless they are generally very tolerant of others on board, have great attitudes about disagreements, and are relatively flexible about change.

But being in such close quarters, your dog can't help but be affected by the state of his crew. A bad mood, a fight with your sweetheart, or a stressful day on the job can all make him feel as if his world isn't right. These life events of yours mean big changes in all of your behaviors and signals, and that can mean big changes for him. In many ways, your trials and tribulations are his, too.

And that's just between the two of you. When you get a new roommate or you adopt a cat from the shelter, he sees immediately that things have changed. He starts to get a little sick with worry as the plot thickens between the players. He has to figure out how to build new relationships, and it will take time to build trust and rapport. Bonds are not formed overnight. In the meantime he might be a little concerned about how these additions are going to add up for him as the numbers rise. Social complexity grows with each of these new members, and all the little things about personalities and relationships can stack up pretty quickly.

Your girlfriend has far less patience for his whining than you do, and doesn't want a dog in the bed. This means the noisy evening games of fetch and nightly snuggling are a thing of the past. The cat gets way better-smelling food than he does, and you won't let him have any. Patterns he could hang his hat on—moments you shared and routines you both adored—have been broken.

It's understandable that your dog could be disturbed by all the challenges and changes in your life. But you might be surprised, and even a little unnerved, to learn just how dependent your dog is on you to be the captain of this ship. And even he knows that without a captain, this ship is going nowhere. He is looking to you for a sense of confidence that you have some idea about what the heck is going on. He's looking to you for the rules, the structure, and the plan.

He has no way of knowing how to negotiate carpools of strange people diving into your backseat, crowds of inappropriately friendly "dog people," well-meaning neighbors who let themselves into the backyard to return a weed trimmer, and an incredible buffet spread on your dining room table that he is expected to completely ignore. His best ideas of how to handle these situations could include a well-placed bite to what looks like an intruder or a grateful gorging on turkey and dressing.

Our job is to create a sense of a tight ship, one that our dog will trust to be afloat at all times. He needs to feel safe or he will be in a constant state of anxiety. While it's not a perfect metaphor, think about how you would feel if you were on a boat in the middle of the ocean with no way to get off, no idea of where you were headed, and no sense of stability or predictability day to day. Most likely, you'd want a captain with a plan.

We need to demonstrate that we have a handle on the whole situation—daily life in the home with all of the members of our social group and the many moods and behaviors those people display. Being aware that even little events affect him, we simply want to show him each and every time that the captain has everything under control. When we realistically don't, the best thing to do is to get him out of Dodge so he isn't witnessing the chaos. For instance, when a grumpy person storms dramatically into the room, we could give the dog instructions to "Come here and lie down by me" to let him know that we will handle things and keep him safe, or simply remove him from the scene so he doesn't have to wonder if he should do something about the tension.

Our dog's family (be it two or twenty members) needs to be understood as a critically important element of our dog's environment. We also need to ensure that his relationship with each passenger on the boat is healthy and respectful. This means rules for everyone on board to keep order and prevent chaos.

Every relationship boils down to a contract of sorts between two individuals. Trust is based on the understandings and agreements about the terms—what the expectations and responsibilities are, what rules need to be followed, where the boundaries lie, what the routines look like. The dance of the relationship between two individuals can be an unbelievably beautiful thing when everyone is on the same page about their own part and that of their partner. In each family, there is an atmosphere created by a collection of all of those relationships between its members—one that plays a large part in your dog's overall environment. We can't control every nuance between all of the passengers on board, but it is indeed our responsibility to have an awareness of the power of family in our dog's life.

In order for us to fully enjoy our dog (and therefore save him from possible misunderstandings and disastrous ends), we must understand the role that his surroundings play in his behavior, and take steps to make him feel truly at home as the dog that he is. It is a constant balancing act to create a life that offers plenty of suitable thrills and fulfillment within a comforting framework of stability. He is counting on us to make the world—the environmental shoe—fit as perfectly as it can.

# The "New" Age—OMG!

"Wow! It's NEW!" We are helplessly hooked by novelty. On a biological and neurological level, "new" things arouse our senses, our bodies, and our minds. Anything out of the ordinary gets our attention and energy. To a point, this is helpful for all of us animals—people, dogs, and everything in between. The natural world is no static place; change is inevitable. We have to be able to keep up.

But change is also inherently stressful. To the body (human or animal) this excitement is the same thing as stress. Whether we are thrilled or frightened by the novelty we meet, our bodies are basically having the same chemical experience.

Since we process the "good" and "bad" stress very similarly in our bodies, we can be totally captivated by these things and overwhelmed by them at the same time. Like blocks stacking up, one upon another, building higher and higher, these excitements can raise our cumulative stress to dangerous levels. When the environment changes too quickly, we may reach our limit and go over the edge for no apparent reason, with our loved ones looking on in utter bewilderment as we burst into tears over the burned casserole on Christmas Day.

When we consider the lives we share with our pet dogs in this magical world of the twenty-first century, we need to pause to appreciate how much of it is "new" for them. Sometimes, like us, they are simply overwhelmed by all of the excitement. You'll find that ordinary routines and rituals can be powerful stress relievers for your dog. You'll appreciate how important some predictability and consistency can be in your relationship. You might even find that for your dog, and maybe even for you, "new" can at times be a little overrated.

# CHAPTER FOUR

# Genetics

Now that you've had the chance to consider just how consequential your dog's learning and environment can be to her behavior, it's time to take a closer look at the nuts and bolts of her basic design—her genetics.

In this chapter, you will learn about these powerful genetic traits and how they might affect your dog and her compatibility with you. You'll get insight into the personal profile of your dog's DNA—her qualities and characteristics, her family history, her interests and hobbies, her ideal education and lifestyle. Knowing what kind of material information your dog's genetics bring to the table will give you a powerful advantage in your endeavor to live happily ever after together.

## The Right Dog for the Job

The truth is, we've all had it a little backward so far. We've somehow overcomplicated dog breeds and genetics and simultaneously oversimplified them.

We get lost trying to differentiate between hundreds of dog breeds. The emphasis on the ever-growing array of "pure" and "designer" breeds creates an overwhelming number of choices for the dog lover shopping for their next best friend. We try to educate ourselves about the dog we are getting; then we commit, often with absolutely no idea what we are signing up for, or what steps we might take to keep everything copacetic with our puppy love. We buy the dog—and the idea that the importance of genetics comes down to "good" genes and "bad" ones. We miss the points we really need about our dog's DNA.

It's not *if* a kind of dog has "good" or "bad" breeding that will matter most in the end. It is about *what* the dog was bred for—what circumstances, what places, what behaviors—and why. These are the things that will tell you the most about *what your dog is*. Though there are occasional "bad seeds" in the gene pool, problems are more likely to arise from an owner simply being unaware of what kind of dog he has in the first place.

Think about it this way: If we try to use a hammer to tighten a screw and end up making a big mess, the hammer is not "bad." A bowling ball is not "bad" for breaking our toe if we try to use it in a soccer game. The point is that differences in design matter, even if two things seem categorically related (be they tools, balls, or dogs). Not knowing—or ignoring—what something was made to do can set the stage for misunderstandings and accidents.

It's hard, but when we are on the hunt for our perfect dog, we can't let love blind us. I am as guilty as anyone of totally drooling over certain breeds of dogs. Some of them are heart-stoppingly supermodel gorgeous and others are irresistibly adorable. We can't help but be attracted to the appearance of certain dogs, and in some cases are literally flooded with a cascade of the nurturing hormone oxytocin when we see their big eyes and squishy baby faces. Despite these understandable natural reactions, we have to ask ourselves the tough question: Are we pursuing the right type of dog for our lifestyle and personality, no matter how amazingly cute his little face is? We could be disastrously incompatible. We might want a social butterfly and end up with a suspicious and protective introvert. We might want a quiet companion for our children and end up with a total circus in our living room.

Also, if we are to live with them successfully, we can't afford to ignore the genetics of the dogs we already have and love in our homes. We have to remember that most breeds of dogs were designed to be a *specific tool for a specific job—not to be our pet.*

Most dog breeds we see today are the result of this utilitarian history; and the relationship between their form and function is inseparable. The appearance of these working dogs is tied to the behavioral jobs for which they were bred. Preserving breeds and their standards means keeping the behavioral DNA that created them in the first place. But few of us actually want *all* of those traits anymore. Most of us just want a buddy.

Thankfully, we can find out what our dog was made to do; then he can be appreciated for all of those natural instincts *and* be our buddy at the same time. We can get to the bottom of our dog's DNA as it is most likely to affect us, and make better decisions about the dogs we choose and how we live with them.

You don't have to become an expert on the hundreds of dog breeds, either. You just have to know about the ten primary genetic breed groups— and the one your dog belongs to—in order to be on top of your game. Unlike the traditional organization of breeds provided by kennel clubs, this groundbreaking, simple ten group system I created follows modern phylogenetic mapping of the canine genome, organizing all of the dog breeds into their original working professions.

The goal is to identify which of the original professions your dog belongs to in order to figure out how he might fit into your life: Is he a toy dog for lap warming? A guardian for protecting property? A herding dog for managing livestock? A bull dog for entertainment? A sight hound for hunting with speed? A scent hound for tracking animals? A terrier for killing rodents? A gun dog for game bird hunting? A natural dog with still wilder instincts? Or is he just a world dog?

As you'll see, this chapter is broken into ten subchapters—each of which takes a deep dive into one of the ten groups. Search the breed box at the beginning of each subchapter to identify which of the ten groups your dog—or your prospective dog—falls into. Note that there are a few breeds that fall into more than one group. In that case, make sure you read both sections to get a full picture of your canine companion.

Even if your dog is not a purebred, genetics still factor into the equation. Being part one parent's DNA and part another's does not cancel each parent's genes out; it just complicates the picture. Certain traits can be diluted or muted, while others might remain intact. One should not assume that all mixed-breed dogs are simply "mutts" belonging to no group at all, when there is clear physical evidence in the *form* of the dog that there is a strong representation of an underlying *function*. If a dog's physical traits indicate that he is strongly expressing the shape of one (or even two) genetic breed groups, then he is more prudently approached as such—if one wishes to be prepared for his intended natural behaviors, provide him the best environment, and set him up for success as a companion.

To think about this another way—a hammer/screwdriver combination tool is still both a hammer and a screwdriver—even if it fails to perform one or both functions very well as a result of the combination. So a Corgi/Bassett Hound is still both a Corgi herding dog and a Bassett scent hound, and will very likely behave accordingly in the right circumstances—baying loudly like a good hound when he trees a cat and having a predilection for herding the children through the house. The results are far from an exact science, but it would be erroneous to proclaim that genetics become obsolete as soon as a dog is no longer a "pure breed."

So how can you tell what your dog is if he is a mix? If you know what breeds he is a combination of, read the sections for those breeds.

If you are uncertain about his breeding or don't see your dog's breed listed, the Dog Key® app (at www.thedogkey.com) can determine which genetic breed group(s) your dog belongs to. There you can use the app test feature to discover what his combined physical features reveal about his heritage and the job in his DNA—even if he is a mixed breed. You can, of course, go a step further and have your dog's DNA tested as well. This can provide a clearer map of the precise breeds in his ancestry (though some expert geneticists will tell you that the accuracy of most of these tests isn't exactly remarkable).

As you read, you may be tempted to read only the subchapter for the group your dog belongs to. While this is a natural impulse, I'd like to encourage you to read through each subchapter because there are dozens of universally helpful insights and tips for living successfully with *every* kind of dog scattered throughout the pages. You never know which little hint you stumble upon will be the game-changer for your relationship with your dog! At the very least, be sure to read each chapter's Key Concept section.

Whichever way you decide to proceed, the rest of this chapter will uncover and explain an unbelievable amount of critical, life-changing information about the powerful genetic influences underlying your dog's motivations and behavior.

# Natural Dog

## "WILD AT HEART"

Siberian Husky

Basenji

## TYPES OF NATURAL DOGS

Akita · Alaskan Malamute · American Eskimo Dog · Basenji · Canaan Dog ·
Carolina Dog · Chow Chow · Dingo · Eurasier · Finnish Spitz · German Spitz ·
Japanese Spitz · Karelian Bear Dog · Keeshond · Laika Elkhound ·
New Guinea Singing Dog · Norwegian Elkhound · Samoyed · Shar-Pei ·
Shiba Inu · Siberian Husky · mixes of any of the above breeds

**You'll fall in love with your natural dog because she's:**

**A FREE SPIRIT—**You will revere her intuitive, instinctual, unchained wild nature.

**INDEPENDENT—**She is not clingy, demanding, obsessive, or needy.

**LOGICAL—**She has more common sense than many people you know.

**You might find a natural dog hard to live with because she's:**

**SUSPICIOUS—**She has a strong sense of self-preservation, is discerning and cautious.

**INSTINCTUAL—**Her wilder impulses can range from inconvenient for you to quite serious.

**SELF-PRESERVING—**She can be difficult to train, confine, and handle as a "pet."

😬 **You might find yourself seeking professional help for:**

🐾 Predatory behavior toward other animals, especially smaller ones

🐾 Not coming when called

🐾 Wandering, running away

🐾 Difficulty when she's confined to crates, rooms, yards, etc.

🐾 Intolerance of being handled and restrained—at home, at the vet, at the groomer's, etc.

🐾 Wariness and defensiveness toward strangers

🐾 Destructive behavior in indoor environments

🐾 Difficulty following directions or responding to training

## Family History

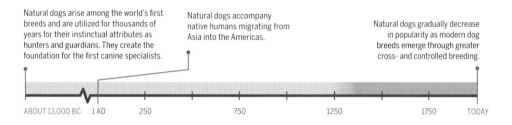

Natural dogs arise among the world's first breeds and are utilized for thousands of years for their instinctual attributes as hunters and guardians. They create the foundation for the first canine specialists.

Natural dogs accompany native humans migrating from Asia into the Americas.

Natural dogs gradually decrease in popularity as modern dog breeds emerge through greater cross- and controlled breeding.

ABOUT 13,000 BC    1 AD    250    750    1250    1750    TODAY

Although there is much contention about the exact dates and origins of the world's first dogs, evidence has consistently supported the claim that the dog-man connection is at least 15,000 years old.[3] Emerging science continues to push the dates back as far as 40,000 years ago,[4] and geneticists admit that the mystery of the first dogs is far from solved. One thing is for sure: The original primitive dogs emerged and thrived because of the presence of mankind, and mankind thrived in turn as a result.[5]

Since the dawn of civilization, humans have told the story of this evolutionary romance in primitive artwork and other tributes to the first canine companions. Cave paintings from 6000 BC depict the distinct shape of the first pariah-like (those original feral and scavenging opportunists) Basenji dogs, with their pricked ears and curly tails.[6] Egyptian relics and drawings of these "tesem" (Ancient Egyptian for "hunting dog") dogs date back to the Protodynastic Period in Egypt (around 3000 BC) and show these animals hunting alongside humans.[7][8] Dogs in art seem to be about as old as art itself.

One may wonder if dogs have been around as long as we humans have. With archaeologists continuing to unearth fossils that place dogs at our side thousands of years earlier than previously thought, we can imagine we will one day discover that man's best friend has been here all along for our own 200,000-year journey as a species.

In questioning geographical origins of the world's first natural dogs, then, it's no surprise that the evidence indicates that the oldest of these

Russian Samoyed, May 1, 1905. Source: *The Samoyed* (New Zealand) (1966, The Cliff Press).

canines arose in the same region of the world as the first humans. The old-world continents of Africa and Asia are home to the same breeds of primitive dogs that split as genetically distinct from wolves. Dogs such as the Basenji from Africa, Israel's Canaan Dog, and the Inuit dogs from which breeds like the Siberian Husky arose, for example, are a mere degree of divergence from their wild ancestors compared to the hundreds of modern breeds we have today.

These kinds of natural dogs were originally *landraces*[9]—populations of canines evolving naturally in a given region without human control of breeding. These natural breeds lived alongside primitive populations of humans, taking advantage of what we had to offer (often in exchange for what benefit they could provide to us). Natural pressures, as well as human practices of favoring given dogs or culling undesired others from their local populations, selected for those best suited to the environments and tasks at hand.

All of these original dogs were, at heart, instinctive hunters and scavengers concerned with the protection of territory. These traits were useful when combined with their reduced fear and aggression regarding humans.

As humans migrated out of Africa, across Asia into northern regions, and westward into ancient Phoenicia, some traits worked better than others. These natural dogs formed the basis for other dog breeds that would ultimately emerge over the course of the next 15,000-plus years, as these early hunters, herders, and protectors were developed and fine-tuned into distinct genetic working groups.

Where these breeds of natural dogs have been preserved, so has a piece of history. While they may at times feel out of place in the twenty-first century, these incredible dogs deserve a reverence for their more primitive ancestry as well as the great role they played in the history of early man and his fight for survival in an often harsh world.

## Upbringing

Bringing up a natural dog is a little bit like raising a headstrong, free-spirited child. You have to give her plenty of room to hold her own and spread her wings. She will not respond well to intimidation or force. Your anger only fuels her confidence and determination. Taking her for granted and treating her as a subordinate will only set the stage for disaster. You have to become savvy, ever-the-wiser, and authentically observant and grounded in order to get *anywhere* as a parent with her.

If you are like most of us dog owners, this is not quite what you signed up for when you got a puppy. You want her to love and adore you unconditionally, hang on your every word, and follow your every move with blind enthusiasm. You want a little darling to dote on and care for, and expect her to eat it all up and get on board. But she squirms away when you put her in your lap. She growls when you try to take her squeaky fish toy away. She seems totally unimpressed with your insistence that she submit to your authority as her human parent. The harder you try to convince her you're in charge, the worse it seems to get.

As with any puppy, this early time in your natural dog's life will establish a template of understandings and behaviors for the years to come. More than with almost any other genetic group of dogs, you need to approach raising her and living together as a contract. Try to think of it as an honor to be a part of this partnership with such a self-assured little thing—lest she grow up resentful and rebellious. You want to introduce her to all of the things that this modern world has in store for her, laying all of the cards on the table at all times. She will live by the "fool me once, shame on you; fool me twice, shame on me" idiom. Trick her, and she will lose regard and trust for you in an instant.

## Interests and Hobbies

Your natural dog is a nature-loving girl who will follow the wind where it takes her. Like her primitive and feral predecessors, she is directed by powerful senses and instincts. Her relationship to the natural world around her—the birds in the trees, the rustling of the leaves, the smells in the air, approaching storms or other trouble on the horizon—can be so powerful that she may seem to disappear into another realm. Don't take it personally if you fall right off her radar. She is far more at home amid the natural landscapes of forests and fields, and all the creatures within them—a world that is increasingly rare in the twenty-first century.

You might be inclined to enroll her in a meditation class for all the time she seems to spend peacefully sitting in silence in a spot of sun. For all the patience and stealth she exhibits hunting squirrels in the yard, you could swear she's been watching your old samurai movies. She is economy of movement, action, and energy in every way.

Your natural dog is less interested in hobbies than she is in endeavors. She is concerned with all that is practical and has little use for anything frivolous. A pioneer dog, she has the well-rounded skills she needs to get by in a demanding world. She will track and hunt, or protect that which is hers, when it seems necessary. She is always pragmatically interested in the more productive means to an end, almost exclusively for her own self-interest (occasionally including those in her intimate social circle). She follows her own internal compass at all times and will heed the summons of the natural world—even in a modern one.

## Education

Forget obedience school. Enroll your natural dog in the school of life. Remember that she can be hard to impress and motivate—even with the best treats and toys on the market. You'll need to get real smart, real quick when you sign up to be her teacher, and to learn how to leverage what she actually cares about. Any energy you spend trying to change her mind will be totally wasted. She was not bred to be a "pet," much less to be "obedient."

But she is your pet. So even if you lower your standards about how well she must listen to you, you will need to find ways to have her handle life appropriately.

As you expose her to things that will likely be difficult for her to handle—critters she shouldn't think of as prey, children with no regard for personal space, veterinarians who manhandle dogs they just met, and leashes that suck all the fun out of things—take steps to ensure she feels considered, protected, and confident in your ability to manage life as it unfolds, so she doesn't take matters into her own hands. Expose her to this kind of stuff without judgment: she isn't naturally inclined to leave vulnerable fuzzy creatures alone nor is she likely to feel like being friendly with total strangers getting handsy with her; she isn't "bad" and you shouldn't feel embarrassed. Make each of those life events that may pose a challenge for her a memorable and ideally positive experience. Your natural dog is paying attention at all times and forming opinions that may stick. Everything is precedent—so you'd better try to make it a good one.

Akita

Hold up your end of the deal in the relationship by conveying to her, "I get it. These things make you feel very out of place or uncomfortable." You can do this by asking her to handle a reasonable expectation—such as minding her own business when walking by the neighbor's cat or holding still for a veterinary exam—and you meet her halfway. You make sure the vet takes it slow and has a nice bedside manner, as you feed her liver bites for tolerating the invasion. You don't walk down that one street with a dozen feral cats living behind the Dumpster and get mad at her when she wants to hunt one. You teach her how smart it is to walk quietly by the kitties at a distance, keenly aware that all that stands between her and her hunting instinct is a well-made leash.

Teaching a natural dog is an art. It requires great self-awareness and introspection, accountability and humility. Connecting with one of these slightly wilder, enchanted creatures can be the kind of experience that fairy tales are made of; and it is also a journey of self-discovery. You will realize, as the teacher, that you are every bit as much a student—whether you like it or not.

## Lifestyle

Life with your natural dog boils down to balance and wonderful irony. She needs plenty of nature . . . with a good solid fence to keep her safe. She needs to be honored for her independence . . . and meticulously guided through the challenges of the modern world. She will not shower you with excessive displays of affection and loyalty . . . and yet you will never know a greater bond. Many different lifestyles can suit her intuitive and grounded character, adaptive as she so naturally is. The bigger question, in many ways, is whether or not her responses suit you.

**HOME LIFE**—If she doesn't like the crate she is stuck in, she is less likely to panic than she is to simply find a way out of it. If she has had enough of your new restrictive schedule at work and the boring late-night leash walks, she will probably just find a way to get out for a tear through the hills on her own when she spots her chance. She will mostly roll with your strange human habits at home, but won't hesitate to take care of her needs as she sees fit. She is the kind of girl who can take care of herself, undemanding and drama-free, as long as she likes the terms being offered.

You forgot to feed her on time tonight because you had an emergency at the office? No problem, don't get up. She will just help herself to the chicken you brought home from the grocery store that is still sitting on the counter. The alarm didn't go off at 6 a.m. so you slept through her morning constitutional at the park? She won't make a big fuss, just a dump on your roommate's bed. Her ability to be self-reliant is convenient when it comes to a time-crunched schedule that does not allow you to entertain her constantly. But it can be a little maddening when she takes it upon herself to solve problems her way.

For her, the answers are usually pretty obvious. The ex-girlfriend with a tendency to drama who shows up at your house at 2 a.m., and who you clearly aren't excited to see? She probably needs to be told to leave. So your natural dog is happy to help by delivering a small snap at the ex's hand as she moves toward you with an uninvited hug. Or the piece of pizza that your nephew dropped on the floor last week—that was obviously unwanted leftovers for her to eat. Why was everyone so mad when she snatched it up? And why on earth would anyone be so rude as to try to take it back, right out of her mouth? She makes every effort to work with you. But sometimes she thinks you just don't get it at all.

The fact that you keep insisting that she lie on the couch with total strangers the way she does with you is totally weird. Would you want to lie on the couch with a total stranger? And what was the point of that bumblebee costume that you got for her to wear on Halloween? It was uncomfortable and itchy, and you kept telling her to stop trying to bite it off. Could you blame her when she snapped at the kid who repeatedly patted her on the head at the costume party and who kept saying, "Bee! Buzz! Bee!" over and over in her face?

It won't be her fault if you bring home a live bunny and it isn't in its cage when you get home. Not only is she good at opening latches; she has a natural interest in catching prey. You can't blame her for taking herself for a long hike when it has been six weeks since you've had the time to go. Don't expect her to stay in a yard with a fence that clearly has a built-in escape route for dogs in the far left corner by the willow tree. She absolutely needs time to follow her senses and instincts outdoors and can't be held responsible if you have forgotten to provide it.

She will make every effort to meet you halfway when it comes to sharing a home, and will be amenable and largely uncomplaining about her circumstances. But she will do what she needs to do for her own sanity—an admirable quality that many of us sharing a home might learn from.

**HOME LIFE SCORE: 2.5 out of 5**

SERIOUSLY CHALLENGING · · · · · · · · · · · · · · · · · · · · THE EASY LIFE

Other than the great challenge of accommodating their needs in the home, natural dogs are among the easiest dogs on the planet to live with. They are fair and reasonable. But we people are still not quite "cool" with loose dogs, hunted neighboring pets, and dogs who protest when people behave "rudely" by disturbing naps and giving hugs to unfamiliar pets. So we agree to disagree, then meet in the middle.

**PUBLIC LIFE**—Being out in public with your natural dog gives rise to special issues, which are best met with an honest, head-on position about the reality of the situation. You will find that she is agreeable to most kinds of activities, provided that everyone else around her is being fair and reasonable, according to her standards.

Your neighbors and friends may not understand her nature and your accommodations to her preferences. They may judge you as antisocial for not joining them at the dog park or chastise you for not training her to tolerate overzealous puppies or the hugs and kisses of friendly humans. Well-meaning people may say things that will cause you to question your own judgment. Ignore all of these voices when you go out into the world. Listen to your own intuition and common sense. And listen to your dog.

Keep other dogs out of her personal space on walks, and she will be willing to stay out of theirs. Protect her from having to contend with socially awkward or abnormally friendly retrievers, and she won't be forced to instruct them herself. Tell other people that she might be uncomfortable being smooched and stroked by strangers, and she will gladly go about minding her own business on the walk.

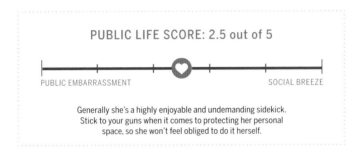

PUBLIC LIFE SCORE: 2.5 out of 5

PUBLIC EMBARRASSMENT                    SOCIAL BREEZE

Generally she's a highly enjoyable and undemanding sidekick.
Stick to your guns when it comes to protecting her personal
space, so she won't feel obliged to do it herself.

**PERSONAL LIFE**—Antoine de Saint-Exupéry once said that "love does not consist in gazing at each other but in looking outward together in the same direction." We enjoy being adored, but what is truly transformative and powerful is the ability to get on the same page. With a natural dog, you will quickly find yourself learning this lesson firsthand. It is a partnership, or it is nothing at all.

Your natural dog will know your emotions and intentions. She will know if you are sincere, if you are scared, or if you are confident. She will be as dialed in to you as she is to the world around her—naturally, instinctually, intuitively. She wants you to do the same for her. She will expect you to be concerned with your own interests, and for you to understand that she is with hers.

Finding your way together in this modern age, far from her ancestral roots, will be a challenge at times. The world we live in expects her to be something she is not—a passive, permissive, and dependent "pet." Your happiness as partners depends on your constant ability to appreciate her for the animal she naturally is, and to meet her halfway.

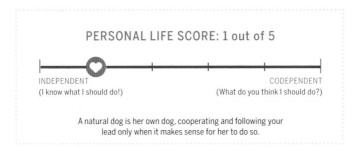

PERSONAL LIFE SCORE: 1 out of 5

INDEPENDENT
(I know what I should do!)

CODEPENDENT
(What do you think I should do?)

A natural dog is her own dog, cooperating and following your
lead only when it makes sense for her to do so.

## KEY CONCEPT: Ritualized Signaling and Communication

One of the most unfortunate crimes of ignorance we have, as people, committed against our pet dogs is the demonization of normal, natural, species-specific communication as "bad." The incredible range of a dog's signals is not only an impressive evolutionary feat, but this great body of messages is their language. All too often, we rob them of speaking.

Because we don't speak dog, we misunderstand what they are saying. The language and cultural barriers between our two species cause us to speculate, make assumptions, judge, and punish accordingly. We do this, quite simply, because we are scared when we do not understand. But so are they. And we create incredible confusion for them when we don't hear what they are saying or react in strange ways to their "words." We even enable misunderstanding and conflict between our pets when we tell them that their communication is "bad," even when it is beautifully stated.

A dog raises a lip when a stranger reaches to pet them—*I am uncomfortable*—and we punish her for saying so. She snaps at another dog for jumping on her back—*I don't like what you are doing*—and we tell her, "Be nice!" The comb catches a knot in her fur at the groomer's and pulls her skin, and she growls—*That hurts me*—and she receives a pop on the nose. We tell our dogs over and over: *No talking*. We pave the way for the moments when they just can't take it anymore, and reach the end of their rope because nobody has been listening to them.

Shiba Inu

The entire point of ritualized communication, signaling, and threatening behavior in nature is to *avoid* actual conflicts and altercations. To assume that warnings are just an indication of intent to harm is backward. Think about it this way: In the wild, there are no veterinary hospitals waiting to provide stitches and antibiotics after a fight. So there are "words" that animals are born with knowledge of and, much like us, learn to speak fluently over the course of their lives through experience. These words are basic language skills for dogs to use and comprehend. When they cannot use them, they are at a social deficit with one another, because they are robbed of their voice about their experiences and feelings. Our dogs are misunderstood and backed into a corner without recourse, simply because we do not speak dog.

So let's take the time to learn their language. They sure as heck are trying to learn ours. We need to value the moments when our dogs "use their words," and teach them that listening to the words of other dogs is the right thing to do. It is what we want for our children. It should be what we want for our dogs, as well.

Natural Dog Relationship Survival Key:

- 🐾 Respect the primitive, wild roots of her **GENETIC** instincts for hunting, protection, and self-preservation.

- 🐾 Give her the greatest gift you can give a natural dog in her daily **ENVIRONMENT**—a big, fat dose of nature therapy in the great outdoors.

- 🐾 Remember that she expects you to be **LEARNING** as much as she is as you guide her through daily life.

- 🐾 Forget yoga and meditation class—get all the Zen you need from your natural dog.

# Sight Hound

## "REGAL RUNNER"

Ibizan Hound

Borzoi

## TYPES OF SIGHT HOUNDS

Afghan Hound · Azawakh · Basenji (natural basal sighthound) · Borzoi · Chart Polski · Galgo Espanol · Greyhound · Ibizan Hound · Irish Wolfhound · Italian Greyhound · Pharaoh Hound · Saluki · Scottish Deerhound · Sloughi · Whippet · mixes of any of the above breeds

**You'll fall in love with your sight hound because he's:**

**ELEGANT**—He's naturally inclined to appreciate the finer things in life, like warmth and comfort.

**RESERVED**—He is generally quiet and calm, unobtrusive and stoic.

**ROMANTIC**—His affection and play are delivered with grace, passion, and sincerity.

**You might find a sight hound hard to live with because he's:**

**SENSITIVE**—He is not cut out for harsh conditions, great endurance, invasiveness, or rough play.

**A FLIGHT RISK**—He has a keen eye for prey and the instincts to hunt it down with sudden swiftness.

**SELF-DIRECTED**—Doting on you or following your directions (particularly, "Come") is often not his top priority.

You might find yourself seeking professional help for:

- Predatory behavior toward other animals

- Not coming when called

- His independent nature regarding your directions and requested "obedience"

- Discomfort with small children and sudden invasions of personal space

- Occasional wariness of strangers or protectiveness of territory and family

## Family History

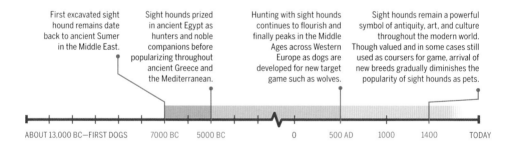

First excavated sight hound remains date back to ancient Sumer in the Middle East.

Sight hounds prized in ancient Egypt as hunters and noble companions before popularizing throughout ancient Greece and the Mediterranean.

Hunting with sight hounds continues to flourish and finally peaks in the Middle Ages across Western Europe as dogs are developed for new target game such as wolves.

Sight hounds remain a powerful symbol of antiquity, art, and culture throughout the modern world. Though valued and in some cases still used as coursers for game, arrival of new breeds gradually diminishes the popularity of sight hounds as pets.

ABOUT 13,000 BC—FIRST DOGS    7000 BC    5000 BC    0    500 AD    1000    1400    TODAY

The world's very first sight hound was a natural dog with a hunting advantage. This original dog—a landrace existing in Africa many thousands of years ago that we now know as the Basenji—was a keen hunter that gradually developed into many of the extreme sight hunting breeds we know today.[10]

These first hunting companions were favored for their speed, as well as for their ability to acutely perceive prey at a distance. As they were fine-tuned for their attributes, the shape of their bodies began to change in critical ways. Their increased range of peripheral vision and incredible

speed resulted in greater hunting success, which in turn caused the structure of their heads to change significantly: The dogs gradually developed dolichocephalic skulls (long and narrow heads with eyes positioned close together), giving them a far wider range of vision (up to 270°, versus the 250° field of view of most dogs). With succeeding generations, legs became longer and chests became deeper, further enabling these masterful sprinters and agile chasers.

By the time early civilization arose in ancient Egypt and the Middle East, the world had its first true sight hounds in the form we know today—long and lean from head to tail. Mankind had also embraced the idea of indoor canine companions, so sight hounds began to appear at the side of Egyptian nobility, and to be buried alongside them honorably in death. The value of these impressive animals as hunters and partners to humans in ancient times is irrefutable, as they were depicted in early art in caves and tombs.

In the Middle Ages in Western Europe, while large guardian breeds of dogs patiently protected flocks in the fields, sight hounds were increasingly used and bred for hunting the wolves that threatened livestock. By the ninth century, wolves were such a problem for humans that there were officially appointed wolf hunters in England and France. The *louvetiers*, as these men were called, were tasked with keeping wolf populations to a minimum, and sight hounds were an invaluable asset to them.[11][12]

In this way, the sight hound evolved as a creature of two extremes— one a sudden sprinting hunter and the other a quiet, reserved indoor companion. Though the dogs were powerful and capable hunters in the woods and fields, humans found that sight hounds were not particularly hardy and lacked long-distance endurance for the hunts.

Away from the hunt, sight hounds maintained a gentler character that ensured their continuing popularity among the elite and noble classes. Today, given their intact predatory instincts, sight hounds are far

PERSIAN GREYHOUND

*The Dog Book: A Popular History of the Dog, with Practical Information as to Care and Management Of House, Kennel, and Exhibition Dogs; And Descriptions of All the Important Breeds* (1906, Doubleday).

from ideal candidates for off-leash adventures. But they are still among the most charmingly refined and enjoyable companions for indoor life-styles. They are as content to lie at the foot of your recliner today as they were at the thrones of ancient rulers thousands of years ago. Given the occasional opportunity to follow his natural instinct to run at top speed or course an unsuspecting rabbit through a field, a sight hound is a highly agreeable dog, well suited to the expectations of many pet owners in the modern age.

## Upbringing

If you find yourself in the position of rearing a sight-hound puppy on your own, you'll want to keep a few things in mind. A more-the-merrier approach to socialization (with both people and other animals) could potentially create negative, overwhelming experiences for your dog. And a sink-or-swim philosophy regarding all of the stimulation of the modern world could put your refined fellow over the edge. He will need to be socialized while respected as the dog that he is—royally reserved compared to many other modern dog breeds—rather than expected to be like his more gregarious and demonstrative wildling cousins.

If pummeled by a sweet Labrador puppy in play group, your sight hound may be aghast, and decide that all other dogs are horrifically dangerous ruffians. Nor will he learn to love children via exposure to your toddler nieces if they manhandle him like a doll on Easter Sunday. The upper-class standing he carries in his DNA is almost palpably apparent as he appears offended by many common behaviors exhibited socially by humans and dogs. Be very deliberate about your dog's experiences, and take it slow, until he concludes his world is a tolerable place.

If you protect him from the rudeness of others throughout his early months and beyond, he'll be gracious and patient with you. Also, do acclimate him, pleasantly, to those invasive and uncomfortable necessary evils that inevitably arise at groomers and vets in the years to come.

His one great genetic temptation to lose all poise will arise when he has the opportunity to hunt. In those first months of life, you should expose him to smaller creatures—dogs, cats, bunnies, and other critters—under *controlled* circumstances in order to introduce them as social counterparts rather than something to hunt.

You will want to prevent any opportunity to chase other pets, as this behavior quickly reinforces itself as his calling in life. Teach him, instead, that the awesome toys you provide are the logical outlet for his natural drives, and get him hooked on games with inanimate objects that satisfy his instincts. Build in a strong "Come!" behavior at an early age, as well, to maximize your chances of getting him back if he slips his collar to chase a squirrel in the park.

## Interests and Hobbies

Your sight hound loves the lifestyle of the gentleman. He can spend inordinate amounts of time lying around in his castle, easily resting in the comfort of warmth and good company. He is just as jolly to rise for the afternoon walk or run on the green before returning for refreshments on the veranda. He appreciates his provisions with few complaints or agitations, provided he's given the chance to routinely stretch his legs and show off his athleticism within the confines of his estate.

He is not overly ambitious about his interests. He is naturally social and amicable, especially within his trusted circle. Cuddling together, playing with toys, and simply enjoying each other's company are all generally satisfying to him. On the other hand, he enjoys his personal space and independence when his companions are otherwise engaged. Composed and undemanding, he is far less dependent than many other dogs.

His independent side can become suddenly apparent should he spot something desirable at a distance. Then you may witness the power of temptation as he flies off into the sunset after some real or imagined target, and feel invisible as you hopelessly call after him. He loves nothing more than the rush that comes with the all-out stride. It is your task to find those safe places where he can enjoy the greatest of all treasures—the freedom to run at top speed.

## Education

At the risk of sounding snobbish about it, I would suggest that you might want to consider private or home schooling for your sight hound. He can be a bit out of place on many playgrounds, depending on the company. Your sight hound can easily become a target for canine thugs or bullies, as well as a walking invitation for uninvited molestations by well-meaning humans, since he is unthreatening and somewhat passive in character. You don't want him to become unnecessarily defensive or fearful if he feels overwhelmed by unsolicited attention and interactions with others. Teach him that you will ensure his safety and not leave him to fend for himself.

Working with him individually gives you a chance to focus on building a tight bond, which you most definitely need. Though naturally agreeable, your sight hound was not bred for cooperative endeavors outside the home, but rather valued for his natural instincts and abilities. He was never meant to obediently follow your directions in order to accomplish a specific goal. At the end of the day, your sight hound will be pleasantly self-directed, with only minimal inconvenience to you most of the time.

Invest time in establishing consistent and predictable, well-managed routines in your daily life together; and set him up for success with the right collars, leashes, fences, games, and schedules. As well-mannered as most sight hounds naturally are, you will have little need to "get him under control" and are unlikely to encounter the same level of disruptive behaviors common in other kinds of dogs (such as excessive barking, jumping, or chewing). A little bit of training and a lot of good manage-ment, one-on-one, with clear, controlled expectations, will go a long way in facilitating learning moments for your sight hound that can make a difference for years to come.

## Lifestyle

As long as you remember to respect the instincts lying underneath your sight hound's otherwise passive demeanor, you will find that life with him can be a total breeze compared with many other kinds of dogs. If you are prepared for his hunting streak and instinct for self-preservation, you can be living the dream, in love with a dog who is well adapted to a pet lifestyle inside and outside the home.

**HOME LIFE**—Sight hounds have a reputation of being catlike to live with, and in many ways that is true. He is happy to waste the day away on your velour sofa or under the covers while you work at the office. You will be greeted warmly when you return—and probably not to any evidence of mischievous doggie boredom in your absence. The neighbors will not have left you a note on the door about incessant barking, and your dog will not appear to have had a nervous breakdown from spending another day confined at home.

Since he was never bred to work long, intense, and demanding days on the job, he won't be chomping at the bit to be a workaholic now. That doesn't mean he is disinterested in doing fun things or using his mind and body on a regular basis. But indeed you can satisfy a sight hound's need for stimulation with far less time and energy than you might with a different type of dog.

He will appreciate his own space and time; and he will enjoy interactions with you and other fond human and canine friends on his own terms. One of his few requests is that he not be exposed to high levels of stressful activity or excitement; which, for some of us, means he is not well matched to our home environment in the first place. A half-dozen kids or pets running around, or simply one really intense personality in the home, can push his sensitive nature over the edge pretty quickly. A critical condition for making a happy home with your sight hound is the provision of a quiet nest that reflects and honors his generally reserved personality.

As long as he is not overwhelmed, he is likely to be hospitable to visitors. He can, like any good gentleman, occasionally take offense to forward behavior or cursory gestures. In these times, he can be quick to speak his mind. He does not intend to be the brute or bouncer; he simply has his standards. As long as your company is good-natured and well-mannered, you should have little trouble.

A fenced yard, or any yard at all, is not a requirement given his low demand for exercise. Just use a leash at all times when you go out if there is nothing to keep him in. As a matter of fact, you need to be mindful of his relative intolerance to the elements, as he is not an outside kind of dog. He is a far cry from the ideal candidate for the "farm in the country" scenario so many people imagine as the perfect home for every dog to "run free." But you should identify a local place and time in which you can release your hound in a secure area (such as a well-managed dog park) so that he can let his hair down and sprint on a regular basis. In between such runs, he will likely be content with the short daily walks you provide.

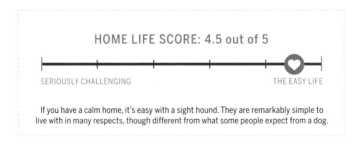

HOME LIFE SCORE: 4.5 out of 5

SERIOUSLY CHALLENGING                    THE EASY LIFE

If you have a calm home, it's easy with a sight hound. They are remarkably simple to live with in many respects, though different from what some people expect from a dog.

**PUBLIC LIFE**—When you are out in the world with your sight hound, you may be astonished by how elegant and poised he is in different circumstances. As long as he is socialized enough to not be undone by its excitement, he will usually handle the modern world with the same calm demeanor he has at home. He will be naturally steady—until some movement catches his sharp eye at a distance and momentarily absorbs his attention.

Even with such moments, sight hounds are almost always lovely to walk on a leash, rarely pulling or straining as they move. Few things are enticing enough to inspire him into action, and the presence of the leash creates a suppression of his hunting instincts. If you didn't know what would happen if you removed the leash altogether, you might be tempted to believe he would simply stroll at your side to the end of the earth and back. But don't enjoy yourself so much that you walk for too long; these dogs were not made for endurance, but rather short bouts of exertion.

As gorgeous as sight hounds often are, you may end up feeling as if you are walking a supermodel down the street as you negotiate a crowd of *ooh*ing and *ahh*ing pedestrians. One of the few great challenges you can face out on the town is simply keeping strangers from doting on your companion and causing him discomfort.

He will be unimpressed with many of the dogs he meets, finding them uncivilized or presumptuous. It is important to bear in mind he is not one for spontaneous wrestling matches with a canine stranger on the sidewalk or bubbly jumping and licking on a first date with another dog. Don't put him in positions he will despise just because owners say their dog is "friendly and really wants to say hi." Just let him keep that pretty nose in the air and keep on walking.

The bottom line for public life with your sight hound is this: Make simple accommodations, and you will find him highly accommodating.

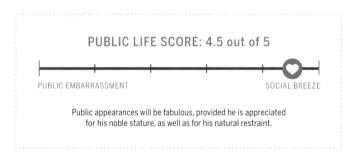

PUBLIC LIFE SCORE: 4.5 out of 5

PUBLIC EMBARRASSMENT                    SOCIAL BREEZE

Public appearances will be fabulous, provided he is appreciated
for his noble stature, as well as for his natural restraint.

**PERSONAL LIFE—**A relationship with a sight hound may sometimes fail to live up to the image people have in their minds about a canine pet. He is unlikely to be the panting, drooling, fawning puppy who wiggles and writhes at your feet looking for belly rubs or another game of fetch. He will not hang on your every word to see if "walk" or "dinner" are in there somewhere. Unless you are ready to lose him, he isn't that hiking or mountain-biking companion you've been dreaming of. Nor is he the dog that many picture their kid growing up with, happy to enjoy everything from slumber parties to camping trips. He is another kind of dog altogether.

For those living a quiet, professional, urban single life or wanting to dance to a slower tune in retirement, he may be the ideal partner. But he does require emotional maturity. With a sight hound, you may be faced with the uncomfortable fact that your own demand for attention and affection is higher than your dog's need for it. If you are one of those people who needs to be doted on constantly by your dog, a sight hound may disappoint.

That said, his expressions of affection are powerful, even if they are economical, and his actions are entirely authentic. A relationship with a sight hound is granted, not assumed. He will, therefore, not necessarily love your new roommate just because you think she is nice. And he may find her puppy to be a complete nightmare and refuse to befriend the little thing.

On the whole, he will be fair and transparent about all of his positions. It will be your task to meet him there and find compromise. Your hope that he will do as he is told or cooperate because you said so will not be effective, and harsh yelling or physical corrections can be seriously damaging to your bond. These kinds of approaches not only fail to convince him of your authority; they will cause great harm to the trust and respect he has for you. To embrace a sight hound is to embrace the higher road of relationship with a dog, the payouts of which are immeasurable.

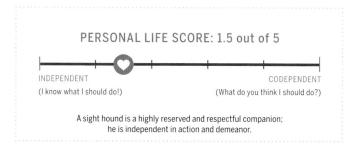

PERSONAL LIFE SCORE: 1.5 out of 5

INDEPENDENT
(I know what I should do!)

CODEPENDENT
(What do you think I should do?)

A sight hound is a highly reserved and respectful companion; he is independent in action and demeanor.

## KEY CONCEPT: Good Management

Good management with your dog is about far more than simply preventing an undesirable or problematic behavior from occurring by means of physical restraint and practical prevention. It is about the creation of a global atmosphere of success through proactive steps. While every dog-human relationship can benefit from the practice of good management, it is rarely clearer than when partnering with a sight hound.

As a dog steward, you are responsible for your dog virtually all of the time. He is very rarely, if ever, responsible for you. This means that *you* get the promotion to management, whether you're really up for it or not. Step up to the plate and get it together for everyone's benefit—for you, for your dog, and for everyone else who will interact with him. You are the one who needs to be paying attention, thinking ahead, planning, taking precautions, and making good decisions.

He sure as heck doesn't know about the dangers of cars on the freeway, or the fallout of neighbor relations and lawsuits resulting from injured pet cats mistaken as prey. The extreme frustration you feel after spending hours chasing him around the park every night when he won't respond to "Come!" is not *his* problem—he might think that you're the one in denial about the circumstances. There are no *rabbits* in his training class, after all.

Sophisticated as he is, your sight hound is all instinct. Don't make your job of living together harder than it has to be. Manage him well.

It's very simple. Think about what tools and other resources you will need to have before you get started, as if you were running your life with him like a business or a project. A martingale slip collar he can't get out of—check. A leash—check. The string around your finger to remind you not to unhook the leash at the park—check. The use of a baby gate to keep your kid from accosting the dog—check. The details make the difference.

A sight hound is a laid-back and accommodating guy who neither requires, nor responds well to, reactive micromanagement. But he does need you to have higher-level control of the situation in place at all times—a constant, unwavering, proactive preparedness for life's circumstances. He

Whippet

isn't the type to challenge you at every turn or stir the soup with drama and manipulation. The benefits of good management with your sight hound will be immeasurable; and yet you will likely never get the chance to fully appreciate what a profound difference your organization and leadership will make. The lost dog, the poor kitty, and the bitten child will never happen—all because you have had good management in place all along.

### Sight Hound Relationship Survival Key:

- Don't take his **GENETIC** design for granted. His passion for independent hunting and sprinting after critters is in his DNA.

- Manage his **ENVIRONMENT** with good planning and decision making in order to set him up for success.

- Create **LEARNING** opportunities and routines that facilitate a strong bond built on trust and respect.

- Treat your sight hound as the regal gentleman he is at all times.

# Guardian

"PATIENT PROTECTOR"

Great Pyrenees

St. Bernard

## TYPES OF GUARDIANS

Akbash · Anatolian Shepherd · Bernese Mountain Dog · Boerboel ·
Bullmastiff · Cane Corso · Dogue de Bordeaux · English Mastiff ·
Fila Brasileiro · Great Dane · Great Pyrenees · Greater Swiss Mountain Dog ·
KangalLeonberger · Komondor · Kuvasz · Maremma Sheepdog ·
Neapolitan Mastiff · Newfoundland · Sarplaninac · Spanish Mastiff ·
St. Bernard · Tibetan Mastiff · mixes of any of the above breeds

💙 **You'll fall in love with your guardian because he's:**

**COOL**—Level-headed and mellow, reserved and chivalrous, he has a low-maintenance demeanor.

**TOLERANT**—He's gracious and gentle, and is patient with other human and animal social members.

**PROTECTIVE**—He will surely make you feel safer home alone or walking down the street.

🔊 **You might find a guardian hard to live with because he's:**

**OPINIONATED**—Discerning and independent of mind, a guardian may be resistant to your instructions.

**SUSPICIOUS**—He can be unwelcoming to those he perceives as threats to the home and loved ones.

**BIG**—His size and strength may feel a bit impractical to manage at times.

You might find yourself seeking professional help for:

- Aggression toward unfamiliar people or animals, especially near the home or your property
- Wandering off
- Not coming when called
- Protectiveness of owners or other pets
- Territorial barking
- Difficulty in training, resistance to following directions
- Male-to-male-dog conflicts

## Family History

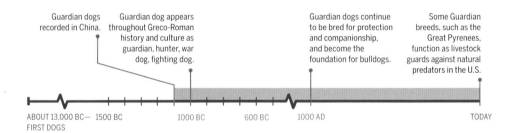

Guardian dogs recorded in China.

Guardian dog appears throughout Greco-Roman history and culture as guardian, hunter, war dog, fighting dog.

Guardian dogs continue to be bred for protection and companionship, and become the foundation for bulldogs.

Some Guardian breeds, such as the Great Pyrenees, function as livestock guards against natural predators in the U.S.

ABOUT 13,000 BC—  1500 BC          1000 BC        600 BC    1000 AD                        TODAY
FIRST DOGS

One of the oldest known breeds, the Tibetan Mastiff, is a member of this impressive group of dogs.[13] Some argue that the first guardian dogs could date as far back as the middle Stone Age, when agrarian societies first found use for such protective animals to keep watch over their precious herds. While possibly dating back much further into ancient history, this large dog was first documented in China in 1100 BC. Sometimes called Do-Khyi[14]—meaning "tied dog"—these dogs were used to protect flocks of sheep, as well as homes and monasteries.[15]

Although records are unclear, Asian nomads are thought to have brought the guardians with them as they migrated west[19]—the very dogs that would become the foundation for the original Molosser (named after the Molossian tribes who used them for protecting their flocks in the mountainous regions of Greece). The appearance of certain livestock guardian breeds (such as the Kangal—a dog originating in the Kang territory lying between China and the Mediterranean) as early as 900 BC seems to support the theory that such dogs were introduced during the journey from their original home in the Far East.[19] It is also possible that other livestock guardian dogs were developed elsewhere in Eurasia separately to assist shepherds in the protection and migration of early domesticated sheep.[16]

As they were traded beyond the shores of Phoenicia, these protective dogs were quickly appreciated for their tenacity in the face of predators and adversaries, some developed into highly prized "war dogs" in Greece and Rome. Wars were won and conquests were waged for thousands of years with these brave and powerful dogs by man's side.[20][21]

As the guardian dogs' hardy and courageous nature became increasingly apparent, they spread across Europe in the first millennium. Other types of working dogs such as hounds and herders were interbred with them for a variety of valuable functions. While they continued to be used as livestock guardians and personal protection both on and off the battlefield, some of these dogs were also later developed for use as castle guards, powerful hunters capable of bringing down larger game, cart pullers, and bull-baiters. Their exceptionally calm, tolerant, and steadfast nature continued to prove very adaptive to home and family protection needs as well, stewards to all that we cared to keep safe.

There appears to be a bit of a paradox within this type of dog. An animal descended from wolves that is passive enough to live peacefully with easy-to-kill baby herd animals, and yet is ferocious enough to hold its own against a Roman soldier? How could this be possible? Amazing as it is, it's quite simple: genetic diversity. An original guardian dog, bred to protect livestock from predators, represents an incredible and fascinating genetic

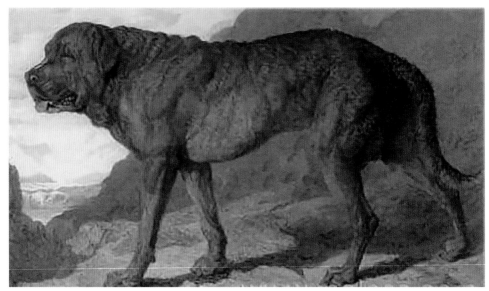

*Untitled*, Alpine Mastiff, 1815, brought to Britain. Source: The late J.S.Morgan, Esq., Leasowe Castle.

divergence from the dogs' predator ancestry through differences in their regulatory DNA (essentially switches that tell genes when to turn on and off, controlling how DNA is expressed).[17] While a proper wolf is a natural hunter with an intact predatory sequence—following through from the initial orient step of the sequence (location of prey) to the end *kill-bite* (killing), and possibly even *dissect/consume* (eating the prey)—a true guardian dog lacks this predatory sequence. He is a lemon of a hunter among predators.

Scientists are still working hard to understand the exact mechanisms by which such a divergence could occur, but many epi-geneticists (scientists studying regulatory DNA) and other researchers believe that the differences in DNA SNPs (single nucleotide polymorphisms) that regulate this *expression* of genes could be responsible for changes such as this muting of the predatory behavior.[18] In other words, the natural "hunter" may technically still be in the DNA "hardware" of these dogs, but is silenced by the "software." The result is a natural predator who will not hunt and kill the vulnerable herds and flocks it is charged to protect. Suddenly, these dogs' reputation as the wonderfully patient and tolerant gentle giants they are makes a whole lot of sense.

This difference was to the agricultural man's advantage—the guardian's total lack of engagement in the predatory sequence has been a blessing for humans as we put his other skills to good use. If he were not so distinctly different from his ancestors, our flocks would not have been safe amid these guardians, but would, instead, have been their prey.

How could these good-natured dogs, merrily living among little lambs, possibly be later developed into war dogs and gladiators in blood-sport events? Again, the answer probably lies in the functions and effects of genetic diversity. It's possible that, by favoring certain dogs historically, shepherds managed to genetically mute the guardian's predator behavior while strengthening his instinctually territorial and protective behavior. A guardian dog's incredible perception for potential threats—his concern about dangers to his territory and social members—is the very nature and historical value of this kind of dog. A concentrated manager of threats, he is cautious, deliberate, and capable when facing any opposition; yet he is no longer the traditional predator he once was. The difference is, somehow, in his DNA.

These dogs' phenomenal physical and behavioral attributes have been employed, admired, and valued for thousands of years in a variety of conditions, and they still are today.

## Upbringing

For those early months of your guardian's life, you would be wise to go out of your way to provide a host of positive experiences for him involving friendly visitors to your home, as well as out and about in the world. That is, if you don't want him to default to his natural instincts to protect your family from your ninety-year-old grandmother who comes to visit the new baby, leaving you to bravely hold granny at bay at your front door. To keep these kinds of awkward moments from occurring between you and your visiting family and friends for years to come, you'll want to take every opportunity to raise your big baby to be relaxed and comfortable with the idea of people in your personal space.

In the critical socialization period in the first few months of your guardian's life, you will have a special opportunity to buffer against the influence of his protective genetic instincts by teaching him how to take a backseat in your social interactions in and outside of the home. While you want to be sure to respect the fact that your pup might not exactly want all of these people to invade *his* personal space, he can at least become happy about a certain arrangement. Expose him to a wide variety of people doing all the weird people things that might set off the alarm down the road. And give him all his favorite goodies as you teach him how uneventful it can all be. He may be a little reserved and suspicious about potential "threats" to his home and family no matter what you do, but you can minimize his protective instincts by showing him that it's all good. Do this by doling out the special stash of super snacks and squeakers upon the arrival of potential adversaries like Grandma, the UPS man, and the babysitter.

## Interests and Hobbies

Guardian dogs can be pretty discerning when it comes to what will pique their interest. Most are not chomping at the bit to play silly games like fetch, and have little desire for what they perceive as unnecessary drama or a waste of energy. They are generally wired to pay attention to a select number of things, reserving their interest for those really important moments deserving of their participation. At the end of the day, your dog's agenda is pretty much going to revolve around the fundamental well-being of his social group and territory.

On that note, he is likely to volunteer himself as household watchman and supervisor, graciously enjoying the goings-on of family life as he patiently scans the scene for signs of trouble. He will enjoy idling his days away covertly overseeing his domain from his chosen vantage point, feigning laziness. When he can rest assured that all is well on the home front, he might humor the idea of cuddling, tug-of-war, wrestling, or couching it with you for binge-watching your favorite TV show.

## Education

There are definitely a few practical goals one should have in mind when considering the education of a guardian dog. There are also some little adjustments you might need to make to your expectations about teaching him. The main points are that he is made to be: (a) *large* and (b) *in charge*. Everything to bear in mind about his education will basically revolve around these two considerations.

First, think about how big your dog is likely to get. Depending on his guardian breed or mixed heritage with something else, he is probably going to be somewhere between 65 and 200 pounds when fully grown. Think about that. Your dog just might outweigh you someday. Things that are cute when he is a puppy—jumping up to say hello, leaping onto the sofa and into your lap without warning, pulling you down the street to go and say hi to your friends—are *not* going to be cute when he weighs as much as your

Boerboel

boyfriend. The fact that he is strong-willed as well as strong-bodied will only add to your frustration as you struggle to stay on your feet and hold him back while he plows ahead like a bulldozer.

His size alone dictates critical elementary goals. Teach him to sit to say hello. Teach him that jumping up on anyone or anything will result in lost access to that desired object or person of interest due to a time penalty in the no-fun zone. The best way to do this is to decisively take him away from what he wanted and hook him up to the very boring time-out spot in the corner where you've smartly left a leash tied off to the foot of the piano. Reward him for keeping those big old paws on the floor. Don't let him hang out on the furniture (at least without express permission) unless you plan on just giving it to him. You will never be able to enjoy a cup of coffee or the newspaper with a great whale surging over your lap, and your friends will probably stop coming over and never tell you why.

Second, make it clear that he has a really great officer (you) calling the shots and that you'll let him know if and when you need him for backup. He actually doesn't mind being the background tank waiting for that special moment of heroism to arise—even if it never comes. He wasn't bred to stir the pot or make trouble; he was developed to take action only when needed. But this is the twenty-first century and you don't have a flock to defend from wolves or an army of Roman soldiers marching into battle. You don't need him to guard the castle from marauding invaders. He will have no idea when his protection is needed or not, unless you show him and explain it to him. You step up and take the wheel. He stands down and chills out in the backseat, waiting for that big moment (which you hope will never come) when he gets to save the day.

If he sees that you are on top of things, he will be content to clock out. On the other hand, if he thinks that you are not paying attention, are feeling ambiguous or anxious, or lack confidence and assertiveness in the face of life's challenges, chances are he will step up to the plate and gladly take those reins on behalf of the team. That's just the kind of guy he is. Don't expect him to *take directions* so much as pay attention to how *you* handle stuff that happens. *Manage him in relation to the events in his environment* in order to teach him (visitors entering, neighbors walking by, other animals approaching his people); use consistent routines and structure to *show* him that you've got this. If you appear to him to be confident, cool, collected, and on top of things (rather than passive, tense, and ambiguous) he will generally follow your lead. Instead of letting him run out the front door to greet your disgruntled landlord, put him on a leash and hand him some treats as you walk out to let him know it's all okay with you (or even put him away with a nice bone in another room while you chat with a particular visitor). When you're going for a hike with your best friend and her dog, ride separately to the trailhead rather than offering to pick the pair up at her apartment and pack the pups into the very small territory of your backseat. Don't give him the chance to take over. Don't "just see how it goes." Think, plan, and give him lots of feedback for doing the right thing (like nothing at all), and take him out of the picture calmly and immediately if he takes action at the wrong time.

## Lifestyle

Guardian dogs are pretty darn flexible when it comes to the lifestyles they can adapt to. They can be happy in the country, suburbs, and city. They can handle sharing life with a person who works long hours in an office or one who spends most of their time at home. Surprisingly, despite their larger size, they don't need a whole lot of room and generally do well in an apartment or condo, given their relatively sedentary nature. In many ways, guardians are not high maintenance companions at all—as long as you keep their basic instincts in mind (and tools in hand) and don't forget them.

**HOME LIFE**—Life at home with your guardian can feel too good to be true sometimes. He is attentive and affectionate without being hyperactive or overly demanding of your attention. He doesn't ask that you throw the ball for hours on end. He doesn't pace around the house in complete boredom just waiting for you to do something exciting. Rather than bouncing off the walls with endless energy that rivals your six-year-old nephew on a sugar high, he spends an inordinate amount of time sleeping on your love-seat-turned-dog-bed. He makes this dog-owning thing almost look easy.

That is, until there is an "intruder." It might be the landlord, your cousin's poodle, or the pizza guy. Suddenly your peaceful nest can feel like a suspenseful showdown scene from an old Western. Worse, it might turn into a scene from a gladiator movie. Your big couch potato can switch into Dirty Harry in an instant—if you forget to be prepared for these kinds of moments.

So tie a string to your finger if you need to, but take a few simple steps to keep everyone feeling comfy at home with your guardian dog. Keep the doors locked to prevent unannounced visitors from barging in. Don't say,

"Yes, the key is under the mat!" when your coworker asks if she can just let herself in when she comes over. Don't offer to babysit for your friend's dog when she goes out of town for the weekend and expect your dog to welcome him into your home (even if they *are* friends at the dog park). And, please, kick the massive puppy out of your bed and put him in his crate *before* you let your new lover under the covers. Or your new sweetheart might receive an unwelcome warning about joining you in bed and decide to go home early . . . and not come back.

You have to remember that your guardian is going to look out for you, and that he will naturally protect the home turf and everybody who belongs in it. All you really have to do is show him that the events in your life— delivery guys, buddies, and all—are under your control and nothing to worry about. Think ahead and make sure that your actions explain to him that it's all good. Don't let him think he has been positioned purposefully between you and "the bad guy." You would be wise to give him a butcher bone and clock him out for a lunch break behind a baby gate when the doorbell rings, so he can watch you extend a warm and confident welcome to your company. If he can see you've got a handle on it all and trust your decision that someone checks out, he can just sit back and take a nap— even if it is with one eye open.

HOME LIFE SCORE: 3 out of 5

SERIOUSLY CHALLENGING · · · THE EASY LIFE

Guardians can be amazing in the home as "pets," even though they are the largest kind of dog you can get. They are pretty quiet and don't need a lot to entertain them, to the extent that you might sometimes mistake the dog for another piece of furniture. Their strong wariness about "intruders," however, can create some pretty giant problems if you don't think and plan ahead.

**PUBLIC LIFE**—You will need an appropriate collar or harness (I prefer a head halter for these small ponies) in order to maintain physical control of your guardian when he shows an interest in something. That said, you might be surprised how easy it can be to enjoy leisurely strolls with such an enormous creature. A guardian has heavier bones, a slower engine, and an overall design for long periods of inactivity guarding at a post. The result is a relatively unathletic and un-impulsive dog who can be an absolute joy to walk with, cruising the neighborhood in second gear. He is not built to be your new running buddy as you condition for the Boston Marathon.

Unless he is uneasy about something, a guardian should be casual and cool in public. Away from the "territory," most guardians are neutral and gracious about other dogs and people they cross paths with—as long as those people mind their own business and show no ill intent. Be aware, though, that he may come to view your entire neighborhood as his territory if you walk him around and let him mark the perimeter. It's not a bad idea to limit his marking and excessive sniffing to the shrubs around your house, and change up the locations and routes you take for your walks on a regular basis.

You may run into a culture clash if he is ambushed by adoring big dogs who he views as potential threats. It can be pretty difficult to manage the "puparazzi" who will treat your giant dog like a rock star. However, it's critical that you risk being rude to people who crash into your bubble and insist on kissing him on his big ol' head. Tell them, as politely as you can, to keep their hands to themselves unless otherwise invited. Patient as a guardian is, he might secretly despise the fame and fondling from strangers, even as he calmly stands and smiles.

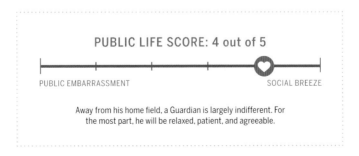

PUBLIC LIFE SCORE: 4 out of 5

PUBLIC EMBARRASSMENT                                      SOCIAL BREEZE

Away from his home field, a Guardian is largely indifferent. For
the most part, he will be relaxed, patient, and agreeable.

Greater Swiss Mountain Dog

**PERSONAL LIFE**—Having a relationship with a guardian dog can be a little bit like dating any badass (even if he does have a soft, big-baby side to him). He might act like he is too cool for school sometimes. He might not gaze into your eyes obsessively and adoringly for hours. It's highly likely that he will ignore you when you are trying to talk to him about something you feel is very important . . . so resolutely, in fact, that you'll wonder if he has a hearing problem. But when it comes to protecting his partner, no one will ever have your back the way he does.

It's a good idea to think about your own personality, as well as life conditions, when it comes to sharing life with a guardian dog. If he observes that you are compromised, unwell, emotional, stressed, or needy, he may feel that he needs to step up to the plate. He may misunderstand the relationship as one in which he needs to be taking care of you. You may find yourself needing to take steps to relieve him of such responsibility—whether it's taking a confidence-building seminar or breaking off that unhealthy friendship that's been stressing you out. Just remember that he is the naturally protective type, and will be hard pressed to just sit back if he feels that you are in need.

He needs you to be laid-back, independent, and unambiguous about decision making if he is to perceive you as a partner rather than a lamb to keep under his watch. He needs you to be one step ahead of him, confidently on top of the scene at all times. If you aren't, he will not take direction from you well in the heat of the moment, and he won't respond well to a challenge or argument. If you are well matched to his disposition and can wear the pants in the relationship, however, you will enjoy a harmonious and intuitive kind of loyalty that has been the stuff of legend for centuries.

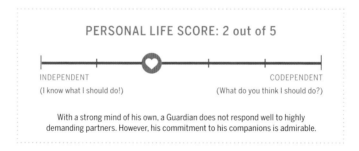

**PERSONAL LIFE SCORE: 2 out of 5**

INDEPENDENT
(I know what I should do!)

CODEPENDENT
(What do you think I should do?)

With a strong mind of his own, a Guardian does not respond well to highly demanding partners. However, his commitment to his companions is admirable.

## KEY CONCEPT: Dominance and Resource Guarding

For thousands of years, wars have been waged in the struggle for dominance over territories and the resources they hold. History books are filled with accounts of men's conquests and crusades against one another. Violent though they are, such events are evolutionarily for good reason. Much is at stake when it comes to locations and property. At the very heart of survival lies the need to protect one's own interest and that of one's social companions and offspring in order to secure a future. Instincts to control access to important individuals, places, and possessions run deep in every animal on earth. And for a guardian, this valor in the face of life's threats is his specialty. After all, such dogs were a deliberate and invaluable assistant in securing and acquiring precious commodities throughout much of mankind's history.

These kinds of struggles for *dominance*—the preferential control of important resources—occur within a social group as well as between separate groups and outside individuals. Animals must be able to correctly assess, respond to, and reconcile any threats to the safety and interest of their self and members. The individual animals within any group with the greatest ability to control resources become the natural leaders—the primary keepers of the realm.

Though there are many factors in the ever-shifting *concept of dominance*, the most stable families and societies are those in which there is a relatively clear *pattern of dominance*. The demonstration of consistent and effective control of meaningful events occurring within and for a group—solid upper management—establishes that pattern. It's about being prepared, making good decisions, and taking decisive action to handle the opportunities and challenges that arise in and for the group. Despite popular conception, though, dominance is *not* about always being first, being aggressive, being bossy or pushy. That's just the domineering pissing-contest stuff that is left when there is no upper management and it's all up in the air. The politics are always the ugliest when there is a seat that needs to be filled.

Your guardian is from original stock chosen for the breed's ability to demonstrate reliable action in order to control and protect resources. It is not a coincidence that this group of dogs are among the most bull-headed about taking directions and have a reputation for needing firm and experienced handling. You don't, thank goodness, need to get in a wrestling match with your 143-pound mastiff in order to step into your rightful and logical place at the helm (you would totally lose). But you do have to control what goes down in the realm day-to-day, so he can sit back and admire how competent you are.

Some of us enjoy the duties of upper management more than others. It may feel a little intimidating if it's not your natural cup of tea, but learning how to be the captain of the ship can do miracles for your confidence (and his). Take stock: Don't let anything go by unnoticed. Have a plan. Take every opportunity to show how thoughtful and prepared you are. Be smart and think ahead. Take action: Step up and put yourself in between him and any "trouble." Remove him if necessary and let him observe from a distance as you handle things. Have policies and procedures. Don't just wing it and throw caution to the wind. Put protocols in place and follow them: *Everybody sits and waits for their dinner bowl or they don't get it. Nobody gets on the furniture without permission or they don't get to be on it at all. Dogs wait in the family room when guests are greeted at the front door and allowed to socialize after coats have been taken and drinks have been served.*

He was bred to pay attention, notice everything, and take action when needed . . . in the interest of the realm. The question he has, before he concedes that he is not most fit to lead this army, is "Are *you* upper-management material?" You had better answer with a firm yes, 24/7. Then he will be happy to just couch it and remain on standby. Infinite patience and inactivity are, fortunately for you, the complimentary attribute of any good tank on the battlefield.

Guardian Relationship Survival Key:

- As you enjoy the pleasantries of living with a more laid-back dog, never forget his **GENETIC** propensity for action when it comes to protecting his home and family.

- Though he can thrive in any number of **ENVIRONMENTS**, remember that you must always manage him in order to stay one step ahead and prevent aggression toward "intruders."

- Help him **LEARN**, through your consistent planning and action, that everything is cool and under control at all times both in and outside your home.

- He is a dog made to do a whole lot of nothing until the moment he decides to do a whole lot of something. Keep it simple and well controlled, and you can enjoy a laid-back, loving guy.

# Toy Dog

## "LITTLE COMPANION"

Maltese

Tibetan Spaniel/Chihuahua mix

## TYPES OF TOY DOGS

Bichon Frise · Bolognese · Cavalier King Charles Spaniel ·
Chihuahua · Chinese Crested · Coton De Tulear · Havanese ·
Japanese Chin · Lhasa Apso · Maltese · Papillon · Pekingese ·
Pomeranian · Pug · Shih Tzu · Tibetan Spaniel · Toy Poodle ·
mixes of any of the above breeds

You'll fall in love with your toy dog because he's:

SENSITIVE—Intuitive and emotional, he is designed for attending to and comforting his person.

ENGAGING—Your toy dog is fun-loving, playful, and curious with family and friends.

PRACTICAL—Highly portable, he is easier to care for, manage, and satisfy than many other dogs.

You might find a toy dog hard to live with because he's:

CODEPENDENT—Your lapdog's clinginess and demands for attention may be challenging.

WARY—Toy dogs may be prone to alarm barking and defensiveness in new conditions.

FRAGILE—Bad weather, exercise, work, injury, or stress can easily put him over the edge.

😊 You might find yourself seeking professional help for:

🐾 Separation anxiety

🐾 House-soiling/difficulty in house training

🐾 His perception of "stranger-danger" at home and in public

🐾 Protectiveness of his person (also known as lap guarding)

🐾 Difficulty with small children

🐾 Excessive barking

🐾 Handling and grooming intolerance

🐾 Reactivity and dramatic behavior toward other dogs

## Family History

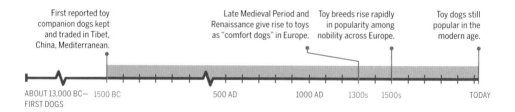

First reported toy companion dogs kept and traded in Tibet, China, Mediterranean.

Late Medieval Period and Renaissance give rise to toys as "comfort dogs" in Europe.

Toy breeds rise rapidly in popularity among nobility across Europe.

Toy dogs still popular in the modern age.

ABOUT 13,000 BC— FIRST DOGS    1500 BC    500 AD    1000 AD    1300s    1500s    TODAY

Despite the popular perception of toy dogs as modern fashion accessories, some of the oldest dog breeds known to man are actually among these iconic canines. Though they are arguably more at home in the twenty-first century pet environment than many other dogs, their story dates back to ancient civilization.

The Maltese breed reportedly originated in ancient Egypt and came to the island of Malta in the heart of the Mediterranean by way of the then-occupying Phoenicians. These dogs were traded in the thriving

seaport of Malta, along with other precious commodities, as early as 1500 BC. This breed was seen as a status symbol in ancient Greek and Roman cultures.[22] The Maltese breed continued to be popular companions to the aristocracy in Medieval and Renaissance Europe, but served other functions as well—such as that of pint-sized flea magnet to improve one's personal hygiene.[23]

Other early toy breeds such as the Pekingese, Lhasa Apso, Tibetan Spaniel, and Shih Tzu originated in China and Tibet. Fondly called "little lion" dogs, these breeds were prized by emperors, and were companions to Buddhist monks long before their rapid rise in popularity among the kings and queens of European nobility in the sixteenth century. These little dogs were literal lap warmers—acting as heating pads and even "sleeve dogs," some small enough to fit in robes worn by members of the Chinese imperial households.[24]

While geneticists are still unraveling the complex histories of toy dogs, there are some interesting facts about this type of dog that can shed light on both our past and our present relationships with them as pets. Many people are unaware, for instance, that many of the dogs in the toy group are actually dwarves. There are three kinds of dwarfism observed in dogs, each having a different effect on the shape of the animal. While some toy breeds carry all three kinds of dwarfism, it is quite possible that *all* of them carry at least one kind—ateliotic pituitary dwarfism—which dictates their much smaller size.[25] In other words, the great variety of toy dogs we see today could very well have begun as simply smaller representations of their larger counter-

"Woman with a Lap Dog," circa 1575 and circa 1600, Florence, Italy. Source: Walters Art Museum.

parts from other groups of dogs. A simple mutation may have resulted in a developmental hindrance that prevented these dwarf dogs from maturing "normally" and kept these dogs little—and we loved it.

After all, who doesn't love a kind, permanent puppy that stays small and needy? It makes us feel so good, so special. Given their incredible popularity over the millennia, apparently very few of us. Any one of us can feel like a king or queen when one of these little lapdogs is sitting with us today.

## Upbringing

Should you have the chance to raise him from a pup yourself, one of the greatest favors you can do for a toy dog is to develop his self-esteem and comfort about being physically independent and alone. Familiarize him with your absence in a comfortable and gradual way while he is young. More than many other dogs, he will need to build up his courage for spending time alone (with some extra pacifiers like cozy blankets and a pile of favorite toys). If he is unprepared and falls apart, you will surely hear about it (your neighbors will tell you that he cried all day long); and you will very likely feel his pain (or the wet carpet under your feet) when you return.

Toy dogs were *made* to want to live in a person's lap (or as close as possible). As a result, the absence of their person can present one of the greatest challenges for a toy dog in a modern age that keeps us humans so busy, and out of the house, for long periods of time. A toy dog, given the breed's ancestral purpose, is inherently more vulnerable to a kind of hyperfocus on and bonding with their person. This can lead not only to difficulty with separation but also to overprotectiveness and hypervigilance about potential threats to his beloved treasure—*you*. Ideally, you will prevent serious problems from developing as you socialize him to a wide range of wonderful friends and promote confidence and relaxation in a variety of circumstances. Bottom line: Adore him but do not coddle him. He is not actually your baby, and needs you to help him learn how to handle being a dog in the modern age.

## Interests and Hobbies

You, you, and you. There is a little variation in the theme: Play with you, walk with you, cuddle with you, protect you, supervise you, help you, etc., but basically it's *you*. If you are one of those people who can't stand a partner that doesn't have a life outside of the relationship, this kind of dog might not be well suited to you. Independent is not exactly his middle name.

While there are many different kinds of dogs represented in this group of littles, they have all been developed for their youthful nature and companionship . . . with *you*. Yes, the distant call of his once-larger heritage will continue to inspire everything from mock hunting to guarding behaviors in your living room. And yes, he will need and enjoy a great deal of physical exercise and mental stimulation just like most other dogs. He loves to play games and knows how to have a good time. He likes to snuggle and watch movies after a gourmet meal. But make no mistake about it: It's really all about *you*.

## Education

Try to imagine what a very different kind of world we are actually trying to prepare your toy dog for, compared to his larger canine friends. More than manners and obedience, he will need practical life skills, as well as confidence in your ability to take charge of events that unfold day to day.

Given his eight-pound size and your ability to simply pick him up if he doesn't follow directions, training him to heel perfectly on the leash is not likely to be at the top of your list. Getting the shivering little guy to urinate outdoors instead of on the carpet in the dead of winter, however, will most definitely be at the top of your list. The inconvenience of his jumping up on your legs or chewing on your belongings will never present the kind of frustration it would if he were a seventy-pound shepherd, but the snapping at your toddler grandkids may be a great deal more serious. It's really a whole other ball game with these sensitive, and often fragile, canine companions.

Safety and comfort (and, of course, you) are paramount to him. Much of his potential "misbehavior" will arise out of his simply feeling *uncomfortable*. Given his small size and emotional nature, he can easily become overwhelmed by the world around him (other dogs, strange people, loud noises, etc.) and overreact to those events. Becoming angry or punitive with him for being upset will only make things worse. You'll have to be proactive in order to prevent him from boiling over in the first place. Step aside just a few more feet to wait out the pack of kindergartners strolling by and give him a little morsel for keeping quiet about the whole thing. Calmly scoop him up before he starts to panic and shriek about the oncoming terrier traffic on Main Street. Be picky about which dogs you allow to socialize with him to ensure he doesn't become overwhelmed by their size and strength. You can't blame such a little guy for becoming defensive if he finds himself in a situation in which he feels vulnerable.

Though not all toy dogs will need such accommodation, it may be wise to provide your toy with helpful aids that will prevent him from feeling unnecessarily distressed. Strollers, slings, and other little dog carriers offer a surprising amount of security (and sometimes even a sense of invisibility) for many toy dogs in busy environments such as festivals or bustling city streets. Teaching your dog to relax in one of these pieces of equipment can be quite valuable.

Many toy dogs are extremely disturbed by contact with strangers, especially children. They often feel more vulnerable and easily threatened than a larger dog might. While socialization to a wide range of people is a good idea, these experiences should be carefully managed to ensure a calm and positive experience for your dog. Don't let anyone reach suddenly, grab at him, scoop him up, poke at him, or otherwise invade his space. Being handled by strangers such as vets and groomers who will have to perform certain necessary evils may not always be positive, but there are steps you can take to make these experiences more comfortable. Work with your little buddy at home on everything from wearing a muzzle to handling exercises; being familiar with (and even enjoying) these kinds of violations of personal space can make the difference between pleasant and nightmare visits for all parties involved. Many of these dogs have greater grooming needs and a higher incidence of health problems than other genetic groups, so they will probably visit these facilities more often than other dogs and therefore could use a little extra help from you.

## Lifestyle

Your toy dog's idea of a perfect world is one of comfort, safety, familiarity, and fun with you. He is a quintessential homebody, and he will relish the little things in your daily routines. His cup is better filled with a trip to the

Phalene Papillon

post office than with a four-mile run. He isn't going to be dying to go out into the big world on his own, and will probably be satisfied with the level of independence that he enjoys when he's exploring a trail within a few feet of you. Lifestyle, for him, is all about the love story of being with you as your constant companion.

**HOME LIFE**—They say home is where the heart is, and for your toy dog this is absolutely the case. He was designed to be happy spending most of his time indoors with his loved ones, and is by far the best suited for small living quarters and a life of luxury. By the same token, he will be miserable if he is made to spend long periods of time outdoors in the elements. Heat, cold, rain, and snow can take a greater toll on him than on many other dogs. Being alone outdoors is probably not his idea of a good time. He is way more vulnerable to predators and even larger pets (which in some cases might include the neighbor's cat). He was made to keep you warm and comfy—indoors. For many of us, this adds up to the perfect "pet" and meets the expectations we had in mind when we decided to get a dog.

But that doesn't mean he is a turnkey, easy dog. He will demand a great deal of your attention and affection throughout the day. He can get all twisted up about things that take your eyes and hands off of him. The telephone, the TV, the computer, dinner cooking on the stove, and your girlfriend can all be adversaries to his fundamental agenda of having you to himself. And this kind of super-clinginess can be a bit overwhelming at times. With a toy dog, you don't really have the option of just putting him out in the yard to get him out from under your feet as you would with another type of dog.

He does, however, need to get out in the great outdoors. He needs exercise and a chance to leave the house. For his smaller legs, a walk around the block can be as fulfilling as a five-mile run for a large athletic dog, which can be good for the time-strapped modern dog owner. He does need it for his sanity, though, so don't get lazy and tell yourself he can get by without his pint-sized adventures just because he's happy to stay at home in front of the tube.

Similarly, just because he has a short stature, that doesn't mean he is short on smarts. He needs to have plenty of interesting things to think about and challenge him just like any other dog. When you are loafing on the sofa or otherwise spending your day at the house, you can spice up his life with toys and games, engaging his active little brain. Turning common living-room furniture into a thrilling puppy parkour obstacle course is one example of something he would love.

If company calls, he can be anything from the welcome wagon to a complete doggie basket case. While some toy dogs naturally enjoy company and strangers (especially if they were properly socialized at a young age), others are wary and insecure about having new people come to the home and see them as intruders. A common behavioral trait of this group of dogs—alarm barking—may emerge when your friends come knocking. While he might warm up after a short period of panic, he is also likely to remain a little perturbed by their presence if they wear out their welcome by simply staying too long. After all, as long as they are at the house, he doesn't have your attention all to himself anymore.

If you make it clear that all this worrisome drama of his is counterproductive, he will ultimately decide it's in his best interest to put a lid on it. After tolerating a brief announcement from him that someone has arrived, ask him kindly to drop the issue: "Quiet, please." If he does not stop barking, first remove him from your lap or his comfortable perch of choice to the demoted position of the floor. If he is quiet, he is a good little dear and again may enjoy the privilege of sitting with you on the sofa. If he is still alarming from the ground, you can excuse yourself from your guest as you remove him from the room and place him on the other side of the gate to spend tea time with the cat instead of you (oh, the very thought of it is so demeaning). If he gets the message and shushes after a few minutes, he can join his cherished best friend again for talk and crumpets in the den.

HOME LIFE SCORE: 4 out of 5

SERIOUSLY CHALLENGING                                    THE EASY LIFE

Toy dogs are arguably the easiest kind of dog to live with day-to-day, especially for a highly indoor lifestyle. But their demand for attention, difficulty with owner absences, lack of independence, and Velcro-dog persona can make them exhausting in their own right. As a result, they score a 4 out of 5 on the home life scale.

**PUBLIC LIFE—**While you are unlikely to have any difficulty holding on to the leash of your pint-sized pup, you may be surprised by how much drama such a small dog can cause as he lunges and barks wildly at other dogs. It is important to realize that he may be very uncomfortable when approached by other dogs. He may get into a bad habit of freaking out simply because he has concluded that the best defense is a really convincing offense. Having the stereotypical Napoleon complex, he may be trying to make up for that smaller size with a dramatic display that would have another dog thinking twice about getting fresh or confrontational. It is worth spending some time rewarding your toy dog for calm and quiet behavior when passing other dogs in order to avoid this common problem.

In general, keep in mind that his easy portability doesn't mean that the great big world will be easy for him to handle. You want to find a balance between protecting him from being overwhelmed and being overprotective. You want him to be able to socialize with other dogs and people without feeling that he has been thrown to the wolves. You want him to be comfortable moving through the world in his own skin on his own legs, even though he does not have the durable and hardy constitution or endurance most other dogs have. He can find great confidence knowing that you have his back and are keeping a keen eye on him as you enter the public arena together. And, hey, if all else fails and the Shih Tzu hits the fan, just scoop him up and move along.

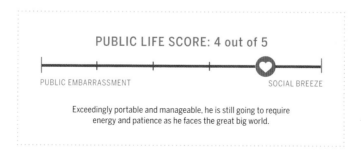

PUBLIC LIFE SCORE: 4 out of 5

PUBLIC EMBARRASSMENT                              SOCIAL BREEZE

Exceedingly portable and manageable, he is still going to require
energy and patience as he faces the great big world.

**PERSONAL LIFE**—Your toy dog's personal life is like a romantic comedy with you and he cast as the stars. It's one part sappy sentimental and one part ridiculous. It's a love story no matter how you slice it—at least in his mind.

You should have no trouble forming a bond with your toy companion. He is a natural romantic, and is far more likely to hang on your every word than to ignore your biddings. He is not scared of commitment, and is born to follow you to the ends of the earth in his devotion. Any relationship problems that arise are likely to be the result of his overprotectiveness of you, and his efforts to maintain your attention at all times.

Of course, this can create a host of other relationship problems in your home and disturb members of your family. For instance, given that you are the most important person (if not *the only* important person) in your toy dog's mind, he is prone to take offense to other pets and people invading his precious space with you. He can become bossy, reactionary, and emotional about the actions of others if he finds them disruptive to his interests. Other pets, interestingly enough, often seem to understand the insecurity behind any such outbursts (or at least find his size far from threatening) and so usually let such behavior slide. This is why many toy dog owners seem to feel that their small dog rules the roost. You are actually more likely to get complaints from your human household companions than you are from the dogs and cats.

Don't underestimate his ability to make waves in paradise. He may be small but he has a strong mind of his own and the determination to go with it—especially when it comes to you. Make sure you don't accidentally encourage his tyranny, entertaining as it can be. You may create a monster you will regret later! Your leverage for keeping things in the personal life running smoothly? Just be clear about what you approve of and what you don't by taking your attention and presence away from him when he acts out. Likewise, pour it on thick when he's keeping his wits about him. After all, he is codependent and looking for your approval.

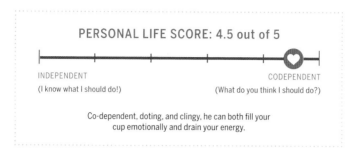

PERSONAL LIFE SCORE: 4.5 out of 5

INDEPENDENT
(I know what I should do!)

CODEPENDENT
(What do you think I should do?)

Co-dependent, doting, and clingy, he can both fill your
cup emotionally and drain your energy.

## KEY CONCEPT: Oxytocin's Hook

Who isn't a sucker for a little animal with oversized facial features and a tiny body that can be held in the crook of our arm like an infant? There is something very real about the chemical reaction that we have to these dogs, an almost helpless urge to nurture and pamper them. When they whimper, our heart strings are pulled. When they stare up at us with needy adoration, we melt. When they follow our every step, and lick our faces, roll over for a belly tickle, and gleefully chase their favorite toy down the hall, we are rendered fools. So we spend more money on their dental plan, more hours preparing their meals, and more energy meeting their needs than our own. How did we become such pushovers?

Oxytocin. This warm and fuzzy feel-good love hormone floods our system when we nurture somebody (or something), and boy do these little dogs flip the switch for us and make good on our care-taking instincts. Our ancestors were likely unaware that they were being rendered helpless by their own hormones, duped into babying these adorable dependent little creatures by their own parenting instincts. But, alas, it worked out pretty well for everyone. These days, we might see we have taken it all just a little too far. When we breed them ever smaller, when we have them believe their own legs don't work as we carry them constantly, when we refuse to cut the symbolic umbilical cord and put them down—we over-baby the baby.

Pug

True, he will never need to really grow up and move out. But if you accidentally foster the idea that he is a helpless infant incapable of surviving even a moment on his own, you might set both him and yourself up for disaster. The tip here is very simple, but the urge you have to fight is potentially very hard to resist. Do not coddle, pamper, and constantly attend to your toy dog's (or any dog's, for that matter) every need as you fall prey to your own "love hormones." Remember that he is not a human child, and that you do him a disservice when you let your maternal or paternal instincts go too far.

If he insists on hiding under your armpit when there is no danger, put him on the floor and ignore his pleadings while promising to protect him from evil granny's uninvited kisses. Pick him back up when he shakes it off and gets a grip on reality. If you close the bathroom door behind you in order to have a few minutes of privacy and he screams as if under zombie siege on the other side, do not acknowledge his desperation, soothe him, or open the door. Wait until he calms down, until the panic subsides and he has been quiet for a few moments, and then invite him in to be with you. If you do not fall prey to treating him like a fragile infant, he will learn how to take important steps as a dog. Remember that he needs you to have faith in him in order to fly. It's your job to gently and appropriately push him out of the nest, so that he won't completely fall apart when life happens.

Toy Relationship Survival Key:

- Cherish but be careful not to encourage his **GENETIC** propensity for dependence on you. It's sweet but can get blown way out of proportion and become a bit of a mess.

- Be mindful of how vulnerable he can be to the elements in his **ENVIRONMENT**, including other animals and children.

- Teach him how capable he is of **LEARNING** the necessary life skills to handle reality, focusing on building his confidence in a variety of situations.

- Remember that he may be small, but he is still a dog who needs you to consider his emotional, mental, and physical needs every day.

MEET YOUR . . .

# Scent Hound

## "SIREN HUNTER"

Bloodhound

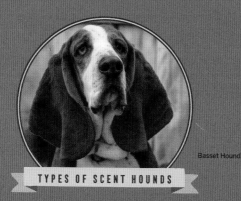

Basset Hound

## TYPES OF SCENT HOUNDS

American Foxhound · Basset Hound · Beagle · Black and Tan Coonhound · Bloodhound · Blue Tick Coonhound · English Foxhound · Harrier · Otterhound · Petit Basset Griffon Vendéen · Plott Hound · Redbone Coonhound · Red Tick Coonhound · Treeing Walker Coonhound · mixes of any of the above breeds

**You'll fall in love with your scent hound because she's:**

**SOCIAL**—She's generally very outgoing and friendly with people and other dogs.

**EMOTIONAL**—She wears her passionate heart on her sleeve about everything, from you to squirrels.

**FUN**—She can be hilarious, playful, social, creative, and adventurous.

**You might find a scent hound hard to live with because she's:**

**IMPULSIVE**—A naturally ambitious dog, she can tune out the entire world and everyone in it when she's on her game.

**A HUNTER**—Her blind (and deaf) determination for sniffing out, tracking, and pursuing targets can be annoying and even quite dangerous to other animals.

**DRAMATIC**—She's born to bay her little heart out when life gets exciting. You may feel like you're watching a pop talent reality show at times.

You might find yourself seeking professional help for:

- Excessive barking

- Predatory behavior toward other animals

- Failure to come when called

- Unmanageability on leash when stimulated by other animals

- Emotional "act first, think later" reactions to threats to space, safety, or other resources

- Difficulty with confinement to smaller spaces/indoor living

## Family History

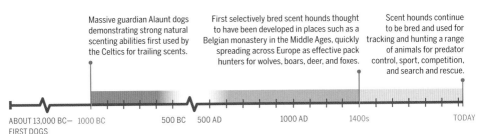

Massive guardian Alaunt dogs demonstrating strong natural scenting abilities first used by the Celtics for trailing scents.

First selectively bred scent hounds thought to have been developed in places such as a Belgian monastery in the Middle Ages, quickly spreading across Europe as effective pack hunters for wolves, boars, deer, and foxes.

Scent hounds continue to be bred and used for tracking and hunting a range of animals for predator control, sport, competition, and search and rescue.

ABOUT 13,000 BC—  1000 BC          500 BC   500 AD          1000 AD        1400s                    TODAY
FIRST DOGS

Thousands of years after humans developed the valuable sight-hunting attributes in ancient dogs, scent-tracking abilities in canines were crafted through selective breeding. Where sight hounds had offered speed and visual acuity, they lacked endurance and steady trailing abilities over rough terrain. When the Celtics found that a handful of early Alaunt-type (guardian) dogs proved to be impressive at following a course and had the hardiness for the conditions as well, the world's first enormous scent hounds emerged.[26]

By the Middle Ages, a small monastery in Belgium, St. Hubert's, had bred a number of dogs believed to be some of the first medium-sized, heavy-boned, long-eared singing hunters—establishing a foundation for the scent hounds to follow.[26] The popularity of these dogs, valued for their profound

olfactory capabilities and resilience under harsh conditions, spread rapidly throughout Europe as large animals (particularly wolves) were hunted
widely up until the nineteenth century in France, Belgium, and Germany.

Over the years, scent hounds were increasingly valued and bred for
"voice" (the characteristic "baying" vocalization that alerts hunters to their
dog's location), unwavering commitment to the scent trail, and their determination to follow a target over miles of difficult landscape. While hunts
usually resulted in cornering, trapping, or treeing the game (chasing the
target animal up into a tree and holding it there by "barking up the right
tree"), many of these dogs maintained a complete predatory sequence and
would eagerly jump in and finish the job when given the chance.[27]

Scent hounds were bred *for heart, from heart*—the descendants of war-
riors with a bold perseverance for the pursuit. The range of size and speed
(from short and slow Bassets to tall and agile Foxhounds) within this hardy
group of large-eared, noisy dogs is the result of man's effort to breed the
ideal hunting dog for different game and conditions. Whether it's a smaller
Beagle or a massive Bloodhound, you are looking at the kind of dog that
was made for the rough-and-ready, impulsive, give-it-all-you-got moment.

*A Year of Sport and Natural History, Shooting, Hunting, Coursing, Falconry And Fishing* (1895, Chapman and Hall).

Though she may be content to laze the day away on the porch, a squirrel on a limb or a scent in the breeze may suddenly awaken the memory of those glorious hunts of the past. Her no-holds-barred, emotional, single-minded response to these golden opportunities can be hard to live with at times. But she should be admired for the dog she was intended to be, even when it is a massive inconvenience. This kind of dog wasn't really made to be a "pet," even if she is one of the best companions you could ever ask for.

## Upbringing

The most critical skill for any scent hound puppy to develop in her early months of life is the ability to *get a grip on herself*. While her brain is still developing, and those little neural pathways are starting to carve out habitual responses to all of life's exciting or stressful moments, you really want to help her learn how to regulate her emotions. This will not come easily to her, being the naturally impulsive, dramatic, and overly sensitive dog that she is. But you can do a great deal to help her out.

First, consider her basic attributes. Her nose and her feelings are built to get the better of her, to consume her attention *completely* despite all odds and distractions. That's what scent hound breeders wanted in their dogs. But it will create some major challenges for her as a pet, and for you as her human companion, if her engine can't be cooled in the heat of the moment. Whether it's baying loudly at the cat on the back of the sofa, leaping at a passing dog on the leash, or running across four lanes of traffic after a squirrel, an emotionally unchained scent hound can be a bit of a train wreck. It's not her intention to ignore you as you try desperately to calm her down or get her back, but it's likely to be infuriating or even dangerous at some point in your journey together.

Your job is to work with the other side of the coin of her emotional nature by appealing to the sensitive, cooperative, and almost passive social nature she can have when she's off the track. As she faces those first suspenseful moments in life, work with her to collect herself as she *starts* to ramp up. Build up her ability to manage her impulses and dampen the furnace under pressure. You can deliberately expose her to exciting smells, people, and places, and to other animals, when she is young, as her instincts are still relatively weak and habits not yet formed. Teach her that self-control and connection to you (like sitting and waiting for a moment before we go say hello to the neighbor's dog) will pay off for her, and that going it alone at full throttle gets her nowhere.

Your scent hound is built like a freight train, building up momentum on the track. You can intervene before she's at a breakneck speed. If you wait until she's full-throttle, you might find yourself sweating it out for a bit. Stopping that train takes time, once it's really moving.

The trick is to find your window. Catch her on the way up. She's easy to read, since she wears her heart on her sleeve. You can intervene constructively as you face all of the drama together. If you learn how to keep her chugging along at a nice steady pace when she's a babe, and always manage her carefully with locks and leashes when life presents too great a temptation for her to ignore, you can avoid ever having a runaway train on your hands.

## Interests and Hobbies

Hunting is at the top of her list, of course . . . and also sniffing, eating, sleeping, playing, cuddling, barking, walking, lying in the sun in the winter, couching it near the AC in the summer. Basically *anything* may be of great interest to your hound. The range of a scent hound's fancies is so incredible, in fact, that some might think of her as a bit of a contradiction. She can be a footloose and fancy free, outgoing, fun-loving and adventurous girl driven by wanderlust and the call of new horizons. Or her feel-good character can make her gravitate toward all the comfortable warm and fuzzy things in life—from snuggly beds to the arms of the ones she loves. Whatever the moment has to offer, the common denominator is her passion for it. She's all about her *senses,* and just plain passionate about being passionate—one great interest at a time.

Your scent hound is undoubtedly thrilled by any chance to chase and tree a critter in the yard and bark with great enthusiasm for hours as it shudders on a limb waiting for her to leave. And yet, she might completely miss the half dozen rabbits hopping about the edges of your garden while she's napping in the sun, so engrossed in the experience of her wonderfully peaceful slumber. She is in the moment of her present mission at all times, whatever it may be.

So while it is true that she is a go-with-the-flow, anything-goes kind of girl, it is also important to remember that she will have her druthers. If something hurts her feelings or scares her—if she has decided for any reason that something is "bad" and should *not* be on her interest list—you might conclude that theatrics are indeed her truest calling above all else.

## Education

There are two primary things you need to remember about your scent hound when it comes to her learning. First, like many of the other genetic groups, she was not exactly designed to follow your directions; she was designed to follow her heart (well, nose and emotion). And, second, those feelings (and smells) that drive her are often obstacles to productive learning. Your job, throughout her education, is to be the engineer of her heart's experiences.

Her heart's agenda is her agenda. That's the genetic code she was built to live by so that she would persevere on the scent trail. Competing with her feelings is useless. You will be hard-pressed to change her mind by trying to sell her on the notion that your idea is better. And getting confrontational with her will only explode in your face—she is a drama queen, after all. You have to value and validate her experiences. Then you have to learn how to exploit them for the sake of the lesson.

So don't let anyone tell you that you should try to make her "obey." Your best move is to show her, time and time again, how totally awesome and resourceful you are at giving her all the good stuff she loves—for a price, of course. You aren't telling her that she *can't* have what she so desperately wants. You're just making it so that you're the quick detour en route to her desired ends. You make yourself the fastest way from point A to point B, asking for a brief moment of her attention and just a little self-control before you grant her wish. The force of her instincts is going to be a powerful river no matter what you do; but at least you can direct the current.

In order to do this, you will want to be one step ahead of her at all times. Shut doors that lead to open opportunities. Use leashes that prevent her from forging her own way. Think ahead, and try to manufacture positive, productive experiences for her that will form the sweet memories and helpful habits you can build on down the road. You don't have to fight her passion, sensitivity, and drama in the process. You can embrace her the way she is, always remembering that she has a heart that can get the better of her in the heat of the moment. Don't compete with what she wants by saying no. Find a way, whenever possible, to say "Yes, but . . ." That's the only way you'll get your impulsive scent hound to learning—by working with her DNA and not against it.

## Lifestyle

To be perfectly frank, scent hounds sometimes have a hard time adapting to many of our modern conditions. It's not that she doesn't relish the comforts of home and the benefits of the easy pet life. In fact, she probably appreciates these luxuries more than most. But her emotional, rough-around-the-edges character can present challenges, especially in highly populated urban and suburban environments. That said, if you are up for the task of fulfilling her hunger for adventure and managing her more unrefined instincts, you will enjoy the splendors of a remarkably sensitive and fun-loving daily companion.

Treeing Walker Coonhound

**HOME LIFE**—If she gets an idea, she is likely to run with it (further, and more impressively, than most dogs would). Much of the time, these ideas are simply harmless and highly amusing: Playing with two toys at the same time, make-believing they are critters trying to get away. Grabbing the blanket off of the back of the chair with her teeth and pulling it over herself in order to make a "doggie burrito." Using three separate pieces of furniture as leap pads to reach the counter where you have left your sandwich. Pushing the door handle down with her paw to enjoy the rest of the house, where she can bark at the squirrels like a broken record before disemboweling your new sofa cushions for fun.

Though these creative antics are admirable (and you just have to appreciate the dog for her humor and boldness), you may occasionally find yourself pulling your hair out as you enter a room to discover the latest fruits of her labor. The good news is, she is probably as lazy as she is creative. If you wear her out sufficiently, you can avoid a great number of trials and tribulations in your living room.

Yes, her "act first, think later" behavior can create some interesting moments in the home. When she sees a squirrel on the bird feeder for the tenth time, she is likely to be so excited that she must tell you "Squirrel!! Squirrel!!" with her excited braying. She totally forgets that you have asked her *not* to bark at the squirrels. You can be doing everything right when it comes to teaching her, and she may be genuinely trying to oblige your request that she *stop* barking just as soon as she can get a handle on herself, but you still find yourself in a pickle when it comes to the neighbor's complaints about her frequent loud barking.

She wasn't bred to be protective of your home, and so is likely to be welcoming to your company. She is generally enthusiastic about socializing, so long as she has had good experiences with people in the past. She can, however, overwhelm certain guests with uninvited sniffs before they've had a chance to experience the more amusing and endearing side of her gregarious personality.

You will find that most people, especially "dog people," quickly fall in love with the naturally sweet and playful demeanor common to a scent hound. Visiting children, in particular, will find her to be a laugh a minute. That said, always keep her emotional nature in mind. She can be quick to say "Hey, that's mine!" about a toy or food bowl that an innocent kid picked up, or be easily upset by a disruption to her lovely nap. Supervising her with people of all ages, as well as other pets, is an important safety net she needs. Don't assume that she will label all dogs and cats as "friend" instead of "prey" just because she has been wonderful with previous animals.

The easiest recipe for success includes a home with a big fenced yard for your hound, where she can safely engage her impulses with abandon. Loose in the country, she will probably disappear for hours on end, if not altogether, as she helplessly hunts down every critter within a quarter mile. In the city, she can function wonderfully if you have the time to exhaust her creative energy appropriately, a good sense of humor, and understanding neighbors who don't work the night shift. The point is that you want to think realistically about what she will be able to control and what she will not, and commit to making any necessary accommodations in your environment, as well as expectations you have in order to suit her passionate nature.

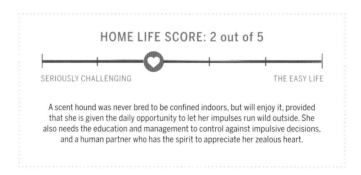

HOME LIFE SCORE: 2 out of 5

SERIOUSLY CHALLENGING                    THE EASY LIFE

A scent hound was never bred to be confined indoors, but will enjoy it, provided that she is given the daily opportunity to let her impulses run wild outside. She also needs the education and management to control against impulsive decisions, and a human partner who has the spirit to appreciate her zealous heart.

PUBLIC LIFE—In public, she will likely epitomize the friendly dog that people adore. She is generally more outgoing and interested in socializing than other kinds of dogs—more indiscriminately affectionate with

Treeing Walker Coonhound

strangers and more interested in schmoozing with other dogs. For those of us who have envisioned a highly social life with our dog, and want to have a canine partner who exhibits extroverted behavior, scent hounds will usually fit the bill.

That said, she can come on a little too strong at times as she eagerly throws herself at the person, animal, or object of interest in her path. She might reflexively tell you that there is a "Dog! Dog! Dog!" over there across the street, and sound as if she is a strangled mad beast as you try to drag her past, your cheeks reddening with embarrassment. Though you may know that the vision of your wide-eyed, lunging, barking dog just means that she's excited, she could come across to others as being aggressive. Her emotions, either way, can throw a little stone in the works of your daily walks.

When it comes to other aspects of public life, such as taking her to the vet or groomer, remember that sensitive heart of hers for the powerful organ it is. She will probably be sweet as honey to all the nice people who feed her treats in the waiting room, and butter in the hands of the professionals she meets. But she could also take that sharp object in her shoulder or stick in her rear end really personally, and react with the intensity of a soap opera diva. Go out of your way to counter the uglier things with really fabulous ones (like feeding her peanut butter while she's getting her exam or bath), and you should earn some positive points for the future.

As long as you do the work to develop her coping mechanisms for excitement and stress, you will most likely find her to be a charming character in your neighborhood and other circles, one whom all wildly adore. Getting a grip and keeping that grip (remembering that you would be wise to never unleash her outside of a fence) on her impulses is the smart thing to do in order to maximize the benefits of having such a fabulous personality at your side.

PUBLIC LIFE SCORE: 2.5 out of 5

PUBLIC EMBARRASSMENT                    SOCIAL BREEZE

She wears her heart on her sleeve wherever she goes, embracing
the moment at hand . . . for better or for worse.

**PERSONAL LIFE**—Your cup will be full in life and love with your scent hound . . . so much that it could inevitably overfloweth and spilleth all over the place. If you can see yourself handling all of that excitement, and are prepared to embrace the character of your hound, you will enjoy a truly unforgettable relationship. You will laugh hard and often. You will never run out of stories to tell about her. You will learn many lessons from this type of dog—about the importance of being in the moment, about going after what you want with determination, and about passionately enjoying all of the good things in life.

In this relationship, you will have to surrender any need to be in control. This kind of bond isn't made for those of us who are type-A, unless we are looking to grow and expand outside of our comfort zone. She will hang on your every word, sure. Until something more exciting catches her interest. You can't take any of it personally—the ignoring of your commands, the running out the door and through the neighborhood, the barking (again) at the squirrels, the masterful acquisition of yet another sandwich from the counter despite your efforts to place it out of reach.

If you can roll with a dog like her, she will go with you just about anywhere, with a positive and jolly attitude. She won't be able to make any promises about her behavior once you get there, but she will try to be all-in at all times. You've got to love her for her renegade spirit and childishly innocent gun-slinging vigor. Her heart is always in the right place.

Though her displays of affection (and really any emotion) can be excessive at times, she is powerfully personal in all of her connections— with you, other family members, and other pet companions. She does need your understanding when it comes to her occasional tendency to shoot from the hip—sometimes dramatically overreacting to perceived threats to her valuables and comforts—but she rarely intends any harm, even in her grumpy moments. She is just . . . so . . . emotional.

Love her for it. Help her through it. Show her how to keep a grip, and forgive her when she just can't get one. She is just as she was intended to be, even if she is a difficult one to love in certain moments. The love you will feel in return from her is powerfully passionate and true to the bone. As with everything else, she gives it her all.

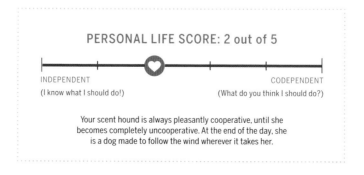

PERSONAL LIFE SCORE: 2 out of 5

INDEPENDENT
(I know what I should do!)

CODEPENDENT
(What do you think I should do?)

Your scent hound is always pleasantly cooperative, until she becomes completely uncooperative. At the end of the day, she is a dog made to follow the wind wherever it takes her.

## KEY CONCEPT: Impulse Control

There she goes. Gone. Good luck getting her back now. Even though she is still attached to the leash you are holding, she is a million miles beyond your reach. There's nothing you can say or do to get her attention or interrupt her blind determination. All rational thinking has slipped away from her. Welcome to her passionate world. Welcome to your scent hound.

She is not broken or unusual. She is not a sociopath, and she has not turned wild. She is just lost in the land of passion, consumed by her own natural impulses in the face of great excitement. She will come back to you, return to being the sweet pup you know and love . . . eventually.

While all dogs can benefit from improved impulse control, scent hounds arguably make the best case for such efforts. In order to make better decisions, take directions more readily, and stay safe in the modern pet landscape these emotional dogs need a little help from us. You'll have to literally teach her body—her nervous system—how to handle all of this excitement better. Helpful as all of that emotion might have been on the hunt, it can be pretty overwhelming on a city block.

First, you want to think about this relationship as one best handled manually, rather than automatically. You need to be able to shift her gears with precision, rather than count on her engine to adjust on its own. Having the tools to slow things down when something stimulating happens will be helpful in preventing her from spilling into her highly emotional and impulsive state. You need only to practice simple steps, such as having her sit or lie down for a few moments, on a regular basis throughout your daily endeavors. Each time you have her sit and chill for a minute before dinner or as the cat enters the room, or when the kids come home from school, or prior to being let out to chase the squirrels on the deck, you are literally training her nervous system to handle life's excitement less dramatically. You can step it up a small notch each day, working up to those larger excitements that seem to really put her over the edge.

Second, you can simply look for and reinforce one of nature's mechanisms for handling the body's stress and excitement levels: *the shake-off.*

You know the common expression we sometimes use to tell someone to calm down and move on: "Just shake it off, man." Well, it's a lot more than an expression. Animal bodies have electric systems (nervous systems), and these systems get "charges" from exciting, stimulating, or stressful events. The accumulation of these charges results in the short-circuiting *fight or flight response*; so animals have built-in ways to release the charges as they occur.[28] Shake-offs are one of these powerful tools that nature provides. The shake-off is a mechanism for calming down and re-stabilizing. You will start to notice how your dog shakes off after he leaves the vet office, after a heated round of play with a friend, after a walk, or after a barking fit at the window. By reinforcing them when they occur—by treats or even praise— you will be facilitating improved life and impulse control skills in your dog, one little shake-off at a time.

Though your scent hound was bred *not* to have great impulse control, all hope is not lost when it comes to helping her get a handle on herself. You definitely have to put in some serious attention and effort, in order to set the stage for success. There are plenty of really exhilarating things in this modern world to get her impulsive little motor running, and you want to be as prepared to handle them together as you possibly can.

Scent Hound Relationship Survival Key:

- 🐾 Keep in mind that she has an impulsive and emotional **GENETIC** nature for pursuit.

- 🐾 Be a proactive mediator between your dog and her **ENVIRONMENT** so her impulses don't get the better of her.

- 🐾 Teach her self-control by becoming the master of "Yes, but . . ." in her **LEARNING** processes.

- 🐾 Treasure your scent hound's heart-wide-open approach to life, without judgment or scorn.

# Gun Dog

### "OUTDOOR ADVENTURER"

Golden Retriever

TYPES OF GUN DOGS

German Shorthair Pointer

American Cocker Spaniel · American Water Spaniel · Barbet · Boykin Spaniel · Brittany Spaniel · Chesapeake Bay Retriever · Clumber Spaniel · English Cocker Spaniel · English Pointer · English Setter · English Springer Spaniel · Field Spaniel · Flat-Coated Retriever · German Shorthair Pointer · German Wirehair Pointer · Golden Retriever · Gordon Setter · Irish Red and White Spaniel · Irish Setter · Irish Water Spaniel · Labrador Retriever · Lagotto Romagnolo · Munsterlander · Portuguese Water Dog · Spinone Italiano · Standard Poodle · Sussex Spaniel · Vizsla · Weimaraner · Welsh Springer Spaniel · Wirehaired Pointing Griffon · mixes of any of the above breeds

♥ You'll fall in love with your gun dog because he's:

**ENTHUSIASTIC**—He is generally eager and willing to get on board with whatever the day brings.

**COOPERATIVE**—A team player at heart, he was made to be an attentive, trainable, and responsive partner in life.

**OUTGOING**—He has an extroverted spirit both with other people and with animals.

⌂ You might find a gun dog hard to live with because he's:

**ACTIVE**—While his ambition for athleticism is admirable, his physical needs can be a little intense at the end of a long day.

**IMMATURE**—The very same silly puppy nature that makes him so playful can also manifest in annoying traits such as a short attention span, neediness, impulsivity, foolishness, or insecurity.

**DOTING**—Though many of us adore the endless affections of our dogs, you may find him a little heavy on the PDA if you really value your personal space.

You might find yourself seeking professional help for:

- Distractibility and impulsivity

- Overwhelming greeting behavior with people, such as jumping and licking

- Destructiveness to home or personal belongings

- Hyperactivity or restlessness

- Sensitivity to loud noises and storms

- Problematic oral fixations, including incessant ball-pushing for yet another round of fetch; sock hunting and consumption; and self-injurious lick granulomas

- "I'll never grow up" Peter Pan complex

## Family History

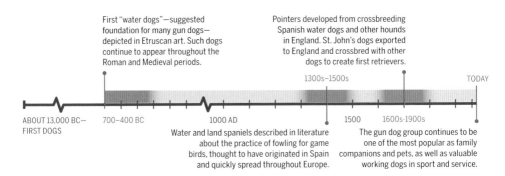

First "water dogs"—suggested foundation for many gun dogs—depicted in Etruscan art. Such dogs continue to appear throughout the Roman and Medieval periods.

Pointers developed from crossbreeding Spanish water dogs and other hounds in England. St. John's dogs exported to England and crossbred with other dogs to create first retrievers.

1300s–1500s    TODAY

ABOUT 13,000 BC– FIRST DOGS    700–400 BC    1000 AD    1500    1600s-1900s

Water and land spaniels described in literature about the practice of fowling for game birds, thought to have originated in Spain and quickly spread throughout Europe.

The gun dog group continues to be one of the most popular as family companions and pets, as well as valuable working dogs in sport and service.

Back when human survival meant making good on any and all available resources, no stone went unturned—including those harder-to-reach food sources in water and air. Waterfowl, fish, and upland game birds all presented potential gold mines for people. But finding and acquiring them presented some problems for humans. Chasing and cornering these kinds

of creatures was uniquely technical—quite different from the direct tracking and hunting of land animals.

When it came to tracking birds, the use of traps, nets, and even falcons helped. But even with these aids, people still needed help finding the birds, moving them, holding them in a location, and even distracting and enticing them. The sensitive winged game targets (with almost endless escape routes in water and air) required a deliberate, patient, and restrained approach to hunting. As a result, humans needed a highly adept and responsive partner in order to get the job done.

Many early dogs were simply too impulsive or independent for the jobs. Persuading a dog to deliver a plump and delicious bird without damaging it (much less eating it) was an impossibly tall order for many an ancient trainer of canines. We had to carefully develop new dogs for these kinds of jobs.

Employing a dog in this kind of pursuit required a level of complex collaboration between man and dog. Here was a critical, unfilled niche in the canine job market. Enter the gun dog.

While the exact origin of the world's first gun dogs is far from definitive, the ancestry of many of these fish and fowl canines can be traced back to the ancient Iberian and Italian Peninsulas, since archaeologists have discovered depictions of such dogs in early Etruscan artwork.[29] The medium-sized, curly-haired water dogs, common along the Italian peninsula as early as 700 BC, were used for a variety of functions in and around the water.[30][31][32]

Such small dogs were probably used for flushing out lowland birds and getting them into nets in river regions such as the Nile in northern Africa, possibly as early as the first century BC.[33] This practice of "fowling" gamebirds by trapping them with the aid of spaniels spawned the first "setting" spaniels: setters.[34] These dogs were adept at not only locating the hidden birds but actually holding them in place by crouching in poised hesitation rather than pushing them out, so that a net could be placed over the birds.[35] Since ancient times, both spaniels and setters have been bred into many different specific breeds, used in various regions for a range of specific hunting needs. They also became highly popular in Europe and the United States as companions.

In Italy, these dogs continued to be popular for their specialized niche in water ("lagot" in the regions dialect of Romagna) up through the nineteenth century. They were later aptly named the Lagotto Romagnolo for their role in water bird retrieval and lowland hunting in marshes and wetlands, until they later became valuable as truffle hunters.[36] In Portugal a few hundred years later, a similar water dog came to make waves—the Cão de Água (meaning "dog of water").[37][38][39] This highly specialized breed we now know as the Portuguese Water Dog was used for herding fish into nets, as well as retrieving nets for the fishermen. Breeds such as the Poodle (Pudelhund) from Germany, and Irish and American Water Spaniels, still exhibit this hallmark curly-haired feature of the original ancient water dogs. Similar curly-haired water dogs continued to spread across Europe, likely giving rise to some of the first known spaniels and setters.

Pointing, or setting, refers to the behavior of a hunting dog freezing, or "pointing" to the prey to show the hunter its location. Normally the hunting process looks like this: *orient-eye-stalk-chase, grab-bite, kill-bite, dissect/consume.* But for this type of dog, a genetic anomaly in the complete natural predatory sequence created a pause in the orient step in the process. This prevented the continuation to the *eye, stalk, chase, grab-bite,* and *kill-bite* steps of hunting, and proved valuable to humans, since the dog would quietly reveal game birds in their hiding places without spooking them. Spanish water dogs (spaniels and possibly setting spaniels) were thought to have contributed to the first official pointers, developed in England by crossbreeding hunting dogs such as Foxhounds and Bloodhounds.[40][41] Pointers have also continued to be developed into a number of varieties, and have maintained a position as popular pets over the years as well.

*The Dog Book: A Popular History of the Dog, with Practical Information as to Care and Management of House, Kennel, and Exhibition Dogs; And Descriptions of All the Important Breeds* (1906, Doubleday).

Historically, gun dogs were not only used in the pursuit of game birds in and around the water, but even for the occasional fish. The most outstanding example of such dogs are the retrievers, developed in England from the now extinct St. John's dog from Newfoundland. This landrace of water dog native to the area, originally used as a working companion to fisherman for retrieving nets, is thought to have derived from Portuguese, Irish, and English working dogs.[42] This "lesser Newfoundland" became the foundation for the modern Labrador, Flat-Coated, Golden, and Chesapeake Bay Retrievers. These breeds were diversified for retrieving game birds both in and out of the water over the years, beyond their original function as fisherman's helpers.[43]

Regardless of their differences, today's wide range of gun dogs all share a number of critical traits as a result of their similar ancestral purposes. They are bred to work not only alongside people but closely in *cooperation* with them—making the dogs highly trainable and attentive canine companions. Gun dogs are also extremely active dogs requiring lots of physical activity on a routine basis in order to thrive. This trait makes them ill-suited to the small quarters and busy lifestyles of many modern pet lovers. This contradiction is becoming increasingly problematic for these dogs in the modern age, as we continue to adore them and struggle to meet their basic needs.

## Upbringing

Think of your gun dog puppy as a toddler, and you will be right on target when it comes to raising him well. He's likely to be a little clingy and sensitive at times, but should also be insatiably curious about exploring, socializing, and having a good time. And he will put just about everything into his mouth.

So, plan on picking up everything within reach that you don't want him to have. And when he finds something—like your sock or cell phone—and proudly carries it into the room, don't make a game of it by chasing him around the house. When it comes to a gun dog, he is constantly trying to find ways to engage you in a game. He will do whatever it takes to get you away from that TV or computer, just like any wickedly smart little toddler. Manage your environment well so he can't get the action started by doing the wrong thing, enticing you to take the bait and chase him, red-faced and screaming, through the house as he chomps on your iPhone.

Be sure to prevent separation anxiety from developing in your new baby as well. Help him learn how to handle your absences early on, providing plenty of special pacifying objects for him to chew on and play with while you are gone. And when you are able to take him along with you, be mindful not to overwhelm him with too high a level of stimulation all at once. He can be sensitive to loud noises and stressful events, so that parade or fireworks display might not be the best socialization experience for him. Don't shelter him from the world or coddle him if he becomes nervous. Just let him pace himself when it comes to all the scary stuff in life, and let his confidence grow one day at a time as you praise him for his accomplishments and courage.

## Interests and Hobbies

For him, life is like a Lewis and Clark adventure just waiting to happen. The eager, wide-eyed, attentive expression common to gun dogs (often confused with a desire to please) reflects the passion for partnership in exploration and work that he carries in his blood from years of careful breeding. He is, quintessentially, ready.

Though it may appear that he wants to do it all for you, make no mis-take: His interests are fundamentally selfish as he seeks to satisfy his own deep-seated hunger for exciting and meaningful moments. Rather than lose heart about this, enjoy the fact that he was bred for the joint pursuit of new horizons and endeavors. His innate ability to cooperate provides endless opportunities to find ways to enjoy life as a team.

After all, this is your duty as his counterpart. He is not just *interested* in going out into fields, woods, lakes, trails, and beaches. He *must*. Though some gun dogs are far more demanding than others, all of them require engaging quests for basic sanity.

Realistically, you may not be able to give him all the in-depth adventure he craves, but you need to recognize that he will fail to adapt to a life of indoor confinement and passivity—especially one that requires him to spend a great deal of time alone. As his instincts urge him to bring you the world (and all the balls, stuffies, sticks, and other items in it), the least you can do in return is to try to provide the thrilling adventures and cooperative missions he so desperately needs.

## Education

Gun dogs are astonishing students—in fact, insatiable ones. Careful breeding for highly responsive assistants in bird hunting selected only the most biddable and ambitious canine learners. Though we rarely train these dogs for their original task, gun dogs maintain a natural inclination to follow directions and learn new skills.

As a result, teaching a gun dog anything from basic obedience to impressively complex behaviors can be a joy. It is not coincidental that many service dogs are chosen from this genetic group, given the need for service animals to perform tasks such as aiding a handler with shopping or laundry, alerting to seizures, or retrieving dropped items. Gun dogs can make the acquisition of such skills look easy, since they are predisposed to cooperate enthusiastically.

The challenge, ironically, is that we often fail to provide enough education to satisfy them. Like any gifted student, a gun dog can become frustrated and agitated by insufficient or unsatisfactory lessons. Chronic under-stimulation of his learning potential can result in disruptive or destructive behavior. Being his committed and passionate professor is a requirement if you wish to enjoy each other's company over the years. Satisfy his thirst for knowledge and development at your side, and relish the vigor with which he participates. It is every teacher's dream to have a student like him.

Vizsla

## Lifestyle

As long as you call yourself Mr. Adventure, you can call him Mr. Cooperative. Intricate involvement in the work, home, and family lives of humans has been a part of your gun dog's ancestry for generations. He will get on board. But that ship had better sail somewhere good every day, and there'd better be plenty of things to learn and do along the way. Bore him and you may regret the day you ever met. Fill his athletic and ambitious cup and enjoy the company of an impressive and endearing partner both in and outside of the home.

**HOME LIFE**—One of the classic "hearth" dogs, your gun dog will be happy to fall sound asleep in the warmth and comforts of home. You'll be able to enjoy your coffee and a peaceful family breakfast on a Sunday morning . . . after he's gotten his cardio on the trail for three hours and then carried the newspaper in for you. If you don't have time for that, he can compromise and settle for a two-mile run around the neighborhood. As long as you make time for a good game of fetch in the yard after you eat, and then take him with you to the hardware store, before the evening swim in the lake.

Given his ancestors' relationships with humans, he is closely attuned to the daily rhythms of his people. He works hard to figure out the patterns, the plans, the expectations, and the goals of the day. He is ready when you are, following your lead to see what's next on the agenda. Keep him actively engaged in your daily activities and burn off his steam with a variety of exciting quests and challenges, and you will find him highly agreeable.

For many, this is actually pretty difficult. Your dog can be hard to satisfy. You probably don't have time to home-school him and run a small marathon on a daily basis in order to please this perfectly agreeable dog. So he easily goes over the top when company arrives—knocking them down, overjoyed to see some action. He eats the molding off the wall because he has spent four hours confined to the laundry room in your absence. He drags your eight-year-old across the street to see the neighbor's new puppy when she takes him out to pee. He paces, whines, and pants as he makes his way around the room from one family member to the other in search of some kind of game or activity. While not bred for protectiveness or home defense and naturally welcoming to family and friends, he can be an unwelcome presence to your visitors due to his enthusiasm. Well intentioned as he usually is, he can come on a little strong for some people.

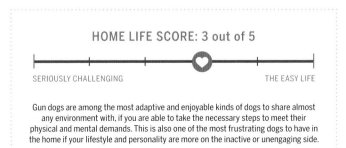

## HOME LIFE SCORE: 3 out of 5

SERIOUSLY CHALLENGING                                    THE EASY LIFE

Gun dogs are among the most adaptive and enjoyable kinds of dogs to share almost any environment with, if you are able to take the necessary steps to meet their physical and mental demands. This is also one of the most frustrating dogs to have in the home if your lifestyle and personality are more on the inactive or unengaging side.

Ultimately he can be happy and nicely behaved in just about any home, as long as you saddle up and take him somewhere, each and every day. The city may be just as good as the country to him, if he has the life of action he craves and is not confined extensively. He needs things to do and he needs you to do them with him, at least some of the time. The good news about this constant demand for your attention is that he will train well, and fast. And, of course, you will finally lose those stubborn ten pounds.

**PUBLIC LIFE**—He is usually the guy that walks down the street and sees every single person and animal as a potential friend and fellow adventurer. His amiable, outgoing, social-butterfly demeanor can make him a wonderful candidate for a highly social neighborhood or a lifestyle that includes dog parks and picnics. On the other hand, minding his own business is not exactly the gun dog's strong suit. This can make for all kinds of awkward social moments when out and about, as he leaps wildly at approaching dogs and children, in hopes of a good time.

So, owner beware: He can get the reputation on the block of being "that guy" to the other dogs. He may be a little too friendly and forward for the old Border Collie next door or the nervous Chihuahua at the corner shop. Telling them, or their owners, that "he just wants to say hi" isn't likely to make them feel any better as he barrels boisterously in their direction.

What's great, though, is that he is totally capable of learning to control himself and be a gentleman. He may have to work at it and fight his urge

PUBLIC LIFE SCORE: 3 out of 5

PUBLIC EMBARRASSMENT                    SOCIAL BREEZE

The average Gun Dog is the quintessential socialite: gregarious and (at times) a little too excitable in public.

to engage, but his trainability and responsiveness to directions can work in your favor—as long as you work at it, too, and fully engage him in the learning process by getting him hooked into your teamwork vibe. Take him on an afternoon hike in exchange for keeping a lid on it when he is downtown. Exercise, educate, and enjoy.

**PERSONAL LIFE**—The "good dog" that so many people envision when fantasizing about the perfect canine companion is often a gun dog. The standard of behavior that we, as a culture, usually hold for our pets is that they are responsive to us, attentive, unthreatening to people and other animals, and a playful counterpart. The gun dog's recent history and culture have played a large part in developing our unconscious ideals for all dogs.

In many ways, gun dogs represent the perfect fit for us as pets, to be sure. They are, however, victims of our increasingly sedentary lifestyles. The changes of the past century—from a largely active and outdoor culture to a primarily indoor and inactive one—have taken a toll on countless relationships between people and their canine companions. Often, our dogs fail to behave in accordance with our wishes only because they are incapable of handling this phenomenal shift. They are deemed unruly, unmanageable, or destructive—all because we neglect their physical and mental activity needs.

If you don't like a lot of attention, affection, interactions, and play, then a gun dog will get on your nerves. His codependency and super-social nature is not for everyone. But if you are truly active and desire a close working

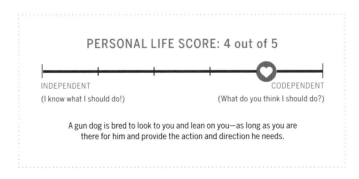

PERSONAL LIFE SCORE: 4 out of 5

INDEPENDENT
(I know what I should do!)

CODEPENDENT
(What do you think I should do?)

A gun dog is bred to look to you and lean on you—as long as you are there for him and provide the action and direction he needs.

partnership with a lighthearted canine counterpart, you will find great satisfaction in this relationship.

Take it to the limit. Teach him to do extraordinary things. Give him purpose in life—a plate to step up to. He will always have his head in the game if you do.

## KEY CONCEPT: Biting

Dogs bite. All dogs bite. Dogs bite lots of different things for lots of different reasons. For them, teeth are more than something to chew food with. Teeth pick things up. Teeth scratch an itch. Teeth are tools. Teeth are everything from hands to a potentially lethal weapon.

Biting another animal socially can also communicate an idea or a point such as "Let's play" or "Please stop." It can bring an end to a hunted animal when well placed. It can injure a competitor or be a threat in the heat of an altercation. Biting is not, to say the least, a simple concept.

Biting is one of the many things, however, we continue to oversimplify. We ask a dog's owner, "Does he bite?" and expect that their answer will clearly tell us if the dog is "good" or "bad." We should all, if we are going to be honest, answer this kind of question with, "Of course, but it depends on the circumstances."

Gun dogs present an interesting starting point for this discussion, as many of them have been genetically selected for certain modifications in biting in order to perform their historical duties correctly. On the one hand, most gun dogs have been selected for a kind of exaggerated oral propensity or fixation. Their inclination to bite things—put items in their mouths, pick those items up and carry or pull them—has been deliberately increased so that they could aid in tasks such as pulling nets and retrieving downed game birds to a hunter. On the flip side, these same dogs have also been selected for a diminished bite—a soft mouth—so that they would not damage a bird's delicate meat by chomping down on it before the delivery.

English Springer Spaniel

So when we talk about dogs, and we talk about biting, we are wise to get a little bit more pragmatic about the conversation all the way around. First and foremost: All dogs bite. It's when and why, how hard and to what end, that matters. Second: Our breeding of dogs for a specific kind of biting (or simply continuing to breed dogs that were originally developed with a specific kind of bite in mind) can have ripple effects in significant ways. Dogs bred for retrieving and for a soft mouth can be neurotic about fetching, but may be less likely to deliver severe bites to a person or animal.

Dogs bred for herding may be far more prone to nipping ankles. Dogs bred to grab rats and break their necks by shaking them with their mouth may be more dangerous to kittens. Dogs bred to hold on once they have bitten may be hard-pressed to let go, though they are less likely to bite in the first place. Such differences in biting between the genetic groups of dogs are not chosen by the animal exhibiting them, nor are they necessarily encouraged by a person's neglect or abuse. In other words, a "bad dog" or a "bad owner" is not required in order to have all sorts of dog bites to deal with.

The conversation about dogs' biting in a society highly concerned with the safety of its citizens would benefit from soliciting the research and insights of modern scientists. We have much to learn. Biting is complicated and must be treated as such if we are to partner successfully with dogs in our homes and communities.

Gun Dog Relationship Survival Key:

- 🐾 Fulfill his **GENETIC** craving for partnership in adventure through games, sports, and outings.

- 🐾 Create satisfactory experiences and exercise in the outdoor **ENVIRONMENT** so you can enjoy the indoors with him.

- 🐾 Provide ongoing and higher education opportunities for him to satisfy his **LEARNING** potential.

- 🐾 Recognize your part in creating a harmonious relationship with such an incredibly cooperative and adaptive companion—grab your hiking boots, mountain bike, or running shoes and get out there!

# Terrier

## "A REAL GO-GETTER"

Norwich Terrier

Wirehair Fox Terrier

## TYPES OF TERRIERS

Airedale Terrier · Australian Terrier · Border Terrier · Cairn Terrier · Fox Terrier · Irish Terrier · Jack Russell Terrier · Kerry Blue Terrier · Lakeland Terrier · Manchester Terrier · Miniature Schnauzer · Norfolk Terrier · Scottish Terrier · Sealyham Terrier · Skye Terrier · Welsh Terrier · West Highland Terrier · Wheaten Terrier · Yorkshire Terrier · mixes of any of the above breeds

♥ You'll fall in love with your terrier because she's:

**DYNAMIC**—She has a big, fun, bold, and witty personality.

**INDEPENDENT**—She isn't particularly clingy and knows how to self-entertain.

**ALWAYS READY**—At the drop of a hat, she's poised for action.

⚡ You might find a terrier hard to live with because she's:

**GOT A ONE-TRACK MIND**—When she sets her sights on something, you may be invisible to her.

**GOT A THING FOR LITTLE CRITTERS**—She can be dangerous to animals she confuses with vermin.

**HYPERACTIVE**—You may wonder if she's ADHD due to the amount of energy she has.

You might find yourself seeking professional help for:

- Difficulty following directions

- Dramatic or unmanageable behavior when walking on the leash

- Excessive barking in the house or yard

- Mischief and trouble making, such as digging up your garden or rummaging through the laundry basket; stirring things up with any family member or pet who she can get a rise out of; stealing things and ripping them into unrecognizable pieces

- Predatory behavior toward animals

- Obsessive spinning, tail-chasing, or preoccupation with toys or other targets like the TV

- Competitiveness or bossiness with other dogs in the home

## Family History

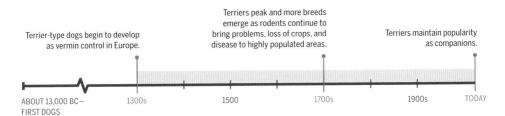

Terrier-type dogs begin to develop as vermin control in Europe.

Terriers peak and more breeds emerge as rodents continue to bring problems, loss of crops, and disease to highly populated areas.

Terriers maintain popularity as companions.

ABOUT 13,000 BC— FIRST DOGS     1300s     1500     1700s     1900s     TODAY

The word "terrier" derives from the French *terre*, or "earth." In a nutshell, their name describes everything about their historically designed specialization for unearthing troublesome critters from their hiding places in the ground. Records date back to the fourteenth century of terrier-type dogs used to hunt and kill animals such as rats, foxes, badgers, and other animal "pests" bothering human settlements.[44] These agile, compact, and

tenacious hunting dogs were a valuable asset to mankind on ships and in fields. Generally small in size, terriers became the ultimate companion in efforts to smoke out critters from their hiding places when larger hounds would fail.[45]

The Enclosure Movement in England, which began in the thirteenth century but saw rapid rise from the fifteenth to the nineteenth centuries, set the stage for the development of terriers as a critical tool.[46] As the landowning wealthy enclosed large tracts of land into their estates to increase wool production and enter market trade for profit, entire populations of subsistence farmers living off of common lands were displaced into crowded cities. The conditions in these urban industrial areas were primed for infestations of rats that would threaten inhabitants and their food supplies. Having dogs who could effectively locate and eliminate these animals was more than a little useful; it was often a matter of life or death. These amicable little dogs quickly grew in popularity across Western Europe, and developed into many different varieties throughout Ireland, Scotland, Germany, and other countries in the region in the nineteenth century.[47]

In World War I, terriers proved to be an invaluable asset once again, this time to the soldiers fighting and living in trenches on the battlefield. In those trenches, hundreds of rats would come to feed off of waste, food sources, the dead, and even wounded soldiers. Having terriers around to keep the numbers down on these quickly reproducing vermin became critical to human survival.[48] By killing off rats, terriers protected soldiers from disease, starvation, and constant harassment.

Long before we humans had the local pest control man to call, we had terriers to do the dirty work for us. Terriers were the right tool for the job, genetically designed for fearless, unrelenting pursuit of their targets, and with the athleticism necessary to carry out the mission. With keen senses and quick responses to the slightest hint of disturbance, these terriers didn't stop at warning rodents and foxes away. They finished the job no matter what, so that the pesky little animals wouldn't return or multiply.

Since then, terriers have been wonderful companions to people, living in and around their homes and businesses in order to protect the spoils within the walls. The terrier legacy may not be for the faint of heart, but it's undeniably impressive for its value to humankind. Each dog carries this family history in its blood today; the terrier is a natural-born "critter getter" even in modern times.

## Upbringing

When raising a terrier, it is important to prepare her for the moments in life that are likely to present the greatest challenges given her vermin-hunting ancestry. You can deliberately introduce her to things like cats, pet rats, other little dogs, running children, etc., in her early months to buffer against the behaviors that she carries in her DNA. If you find yourself with a terrier baby, your primary goal beyond basic socialization should be to raise her to think that other small animals are NOT the target of her instincts. Instead show her how the dozens (yes, dozens) of stuffed animals you bring home for her to disembowel are the proper subjects on which she may unleash her wrath.

*The New Book of the Dog: A Comprehensive Natural History Of British Dogs And Their Foreign Relatives, With Chapters On Law, Breeding, Kennel Management, And Veterinary Treatment* (1907, Cassell).

## Interests and Hobbies

Your terrier is totally turned on by fast-moving objects and small fuzzy squeaking things. The smell, sound, or sight of rodents and other similar critters is extremely exciting to her. She lives for the opportunity of a good chase or the prospect of a little competition. Welcoming a good challenge, she is skilled at both physical and mental debate.

She loves puzzles, games, and problems to solve of almost every variety. Her generally strong and athletic design inspires a passion for engaging exercise that includes obstacles and complex stunts. She is driven to hard work and persistence, and is focused and intense about the activities she enjoys. To be happy, she needs plenty of outlets for her tenacious spirit as well as opportunities for meeting new challenges. These things are meaningful to her on a deep genetic level.

## Education

The terrier was not exactly bred to follow your instructions. While some kinds of dogs historically worked in tandem with people in order to accomplish a goal, terriers were perfected to do their pest-control duties 24/7 with no help (or advice) from us. So your dog is not likely to be the bid-dable little girl you might have imagined, though that doesn't mean she is untrainable. She is smart, cunning, and perceptive. She will learn anything new very quickly. And she will unlearn it the very next day when conditions change and she finds a loophole you didn't count on.

If you send her off to boarding school, she will probably learn how to behave well for the teacher, and then return to her original patterns of behavior as soon as she gets home. There is no way around this fact: You will have to treat every single moment as a learning moment. You need to stay one step ahead of her. She is the class clown, capable of turning the room into a circus in an instant. Your leverage is to be the fun—to be the condition on which every exciting thing happens—and you'll have to hang up the idea that she will respond to the notion of "because I said so." Sew up the loopholes so she can't get around you to get the stuff she wants, and then require cooperation and adherence to certain rules in order for her to gain access to the party.

## Lifestyle

Your terrier's ideal environment is one in which she is close to you, but free to be her own dog, driven daily by opportunities to intensely engage with her surroundings. She is not an idle dog, but can accommodate any number of environments and living situations as long as she is afforded ample occasions for the expression of her character.

**HOME LIFE**—At home she is a lively and often exhausting pet, but a manageable one. She doesn't mind the indoors or periods of confinement, and her generally smaller size makes it easy for her to find smaller quarters (such as your urban condo) agreeable. She can handle your modern schedule as long as you give her lots of amazing outlets for her playful and mischievous instincts, as well as time for adventures and games (lest she dig to China in your flower bed for entertainment).

Jack Russell Terrier

If you live in the suburbs or a city, she would adore a fenced yard in which she can chase squirrels and birds, and dig after moles and grubs. Modern leash requirements in most communities dictate that she not run the neighborhood and torment other pets and wildlife. If you don't have a yard as an option and wish to keep your sanity with a young terrier in your life, you had better plan on an active lifestyle with plenty of action (think in terms of miles, not city blocks, for daily walks). Likewise, she is very well suited to a rural home where she can self-entertain in the outdoors.

Make a point to buy her appropriate toys and don't be shocked when she shreds them into a thousand pieces. Give her your leftover cardboard boxes and plastic soda bottles to murder (supervising to ensure that any little pieces get tossed out and not swallowed, as you would with any other toy). Put her meals into a puzzle food dispenser that she will have to work her little tail off to get into, rather than putting food in a bowl. Use flirt poles and fetch games to help her dial into her chase drive. Animate stuffed toys as if you were performing a ridiculous puppet show and then watch her attack the performers. Tap into your inner kid, get mischievous, and embrace and direct her tenacity in any way you can.

She isn't characteristically stressed by company in the home, as her instincts were never developed for personal protection; so you aren't likely to have the visitor issues common to other kinds of dogs (though she may be so obnoxiously enthusiastic that you wish you'd left her in the bedroom). She may find a hundred ways to be habitually annoying in the house (barking at a certain commercial, incessantly throwing the ball at your feet, digging in the sofa, chasing the cat), but most of these behaviors only pose a small inconvenience as long as you have a personality that is compatible with her general spirit.

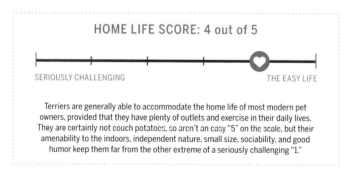

## HOME LIFE SCORE: 4 out of 5

SERIOUSLY CHALLENGING                    THE EASY LIFE

Terriers are generally able to accommodate the home life of most modern pet owners, provided that they have plenty of outlets and exercise in their daily lives. They are certainly not couch potatoes, so aren't an easy "5" on the scale, but their amenability to the indoors, independent nature, small size, sociability, and good humor keep them far from the other extreme of a seriously challenging "1."

**PUBLIC LIFE**—You might find yourself occasionally holding on for dear life when you venture out into the world with your terrier. She is excitable by definition, and the world is an exciting place! This doesn't mean she can't learn how to control herself in a variety of situations, but it isn't exactly a hitch-free process. The sight of a passing dog on the walk or the neighborhood kids on skateboards can put her over the edge in an instant, potentially causing some real drama and embarrassment for you as she barks and spins at the end of the leash. Take your patience with you when you leave the house.

If she has been properly socialized, she will generally love the public arena, enthusiastic and confident as she naturally is. She will not hesitate, however, to respond to an invasion of personal space or liberties taken by other dogs, people, and kids. She is quick to the draw on all accounts, and she should be regarded as such when you navigate the sidewalks and roads with her. It is completely possible for her to be merrily approaching someone one moment and then snapping at them the next if she is uncomfortable. She is not likely to hesitate, so it's a good idea to hesitate for her as your make decisions about how she will interact with the greater world when you go out.

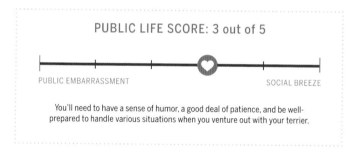

PUBLIC LIFE SCORE: 3 out of 5

PUBLIC EMBARRASSMENT                               SOCIAL BREEZE

You'll need to have a sense of humor, a good deal of patience, and be well-prepared to handle various situations when you venture out with your terrier.

**PERSONAL LIFE**—There are two things to remember when it comes to your terrier's relationship with you or anyone else. First, she is quick to react and can do so without any thought or intention whatsoever. Second, she can be way too smart for her own good. If you take her at face value and recognize that she is not trying to be "bad," you can avoid the common pitfalls in human-terrier relationships and enjoy her many finer qualities.

When it comes to other pets in the home, her emotional quick-draw reactions can spell disaster. The cat she was friends with when it was lying on the bed may suddenly appear to be a target as it streaks through the yard. When your other dog, who is usually her best friend, finds a dead bird on the porch, she might launch into a fight in order to get it. You come home one day to find the hamster cage (and the hamster) in pieces all over your son's bedroom floor because he accidentally left the door open. Expect her to act first, and think later. Use baby gates, doors, and a good dose of thought to keep her out of trouble.

As a wonderful paradox to this, she can seem to spend an inordinate amount of time planning her next move when it comes to manipulating the behavior of others in her social group. She is observant and notices everything. She knows exactly where the lines are, and where they are not. She doesn't hesitate to stretch the gray areas and push the envelope. Her "try, try, try" life mantra and perception for weak spots in the fence can make her tiresome to live with if you take it personally.

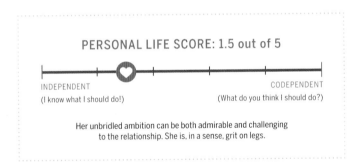

**PERSONAL LIFE SCORE: 1.5 out of 5**

INDEPENDENT
(I know what I should do!)

CODEPENDENT
(What do you think I should do?)

Her unbridled ambition can be both admirable and challenging
to the relationship. She is, in a sense, grit on legs.

## KEY CONCEPT: The Premack Principle

The Premack Principle, the relativity theory of reinforcement developed by psychologist David Premack in 1959, is arguably the most powerful tool you can employ when it comes to controlling your dog's behavior. Terriers exemplify the need for such leverage, since they are hardwired to pursue their goals independently despite our wishes. If you don't want to be left in the dust while your dog passionately follows her ambition down the street, you would be wise to learn about the Premack Principle.

The trick is to take the motivation that is distracting your dog and *exploit* it rather than *compete* with it. Otherwise, you will just get trumped by squirrels and loose dogs at the park as you fall entirely off of your dog's radar. You will never take a natural motivation out of your dog. Instead, you need to answer it and exploit it. Punishing a drive only suppresses it and stores it for a later day. Put yourself in the middle of the equation, rather than outside of it, and show your dog how to get what she wants—by *listening* to you. Here is how this works:

You will require an apparently counterintuitive behavior (like coming) in order for your dog to get something that she wants (such as the squirrel). The idea you are teaching her is that she will fail to chase the squirrel if she pursues it on her own, but may successfully chase it if she goes *through* you first. To do this, you need to prevent her from chasing the squirrel against your wishes.

What you do: Use a long leash as you walk through the park every day. When she sees a squirrel, you give her only enough slack to watch the squirrel from across the way and to feel as if you are a distant thought on the end of the leash. From ten feet behind her, you simply say her name periodically, calling her to you without pulling the leash or admonishing her for ignoring you (which she totally will at first). You get no closer to the squirrel and no further, and neither does she.

After some time, unable to get closer to the squirrel, she will eventually come back to you in exasperation with your stubborn refusal to move. As soon as she does that, you say, "*Yeah!!!*" Then, gently—and very briefly—take her collar before saying "*Okay!!!*" and let it go, as you *chase the squirrel across the park with her* on the long leash. The take-home message for her is that coming to you resulted in squirrel chasing, while ignoring you totally failed. You showed her a new path from point A to point B—she must pass point C (you) first.

At this point, you are probably wondering if she actually has to get the squirrel for this to work. The answer, thankfully, is no. As a matter of fact,

Border Terrier

*chasing* the squirrel is more rewarding to her (brain chemistry going off like the Fourth of July) than *getting* the squirrel (brain chemistry starts to de-escalate upon capture). So you get to pocket the power of the squirrel as a distraction without endangering a single life.

You may also be wondering if you will have encouraged squirrel chasing when all this time you have been trying to get her to ignore them. Remember that *you can't take a natural motivation out of your dog.* The idea, then, is to recognize those motivations and be able to control your dog in the face of them. You get to maintain the necessary control under those high distractions and earn a thousand cool points from her for joining in on the fun rather than continually squashing it.

In order for the Premack Principle to really make a difference, you will need to use it frequently so that your dog can wrap her head around how it works. By definition, the Premack Principle is counterintuitive. It makes a very unlikely action (leaving the squirrel) the actual requirement for a satisfying result (getting the squirrel). It can take quite a few experiences for your terrier to put the pattern together and actually buy into such a preposterous idea, especially when *her* way has worked well for her in the past.

Terrier Relationship Survival Key:

- Manage her **GENETIC** impulses. Be very cautious when she is around small animals, in light of her historical design.

- Exercise her brain and body with complex activities, puzzles, and other challenges and be mindful of her hair-trigger reactions to excitement in the **ENVIRONMENT**.

- Don't get mad, get smart about her **LEARNING**. Work *with* her to show her how to get what she wants the right way; working against her interests is totally futile.

- Have patience and a sense of humor—you'll need them.

# Bull Dog

## "THE ENTERTAINER"

American Staffordshire Terrier

Bull Terrier

**TYPES OF BULL DOGS**

Alapaha Blue Blood Bulldog · American Bulldog · American Staffordshire Terrier · Boxer · Bullmastiff · Bull Terrier · Dogo Argentino · English Bulldog · French Bulldog · Olde English Bulldogge · Pit Bull Terrier · mixes of any of the above

You'll fall in love with your bull dog because he's:

**AFFECTIONATE**—He is naturally engaging, tolerant, and endearing with people.

**ENTERTAINING**—Whether high octane or low, he is a naturally amusing character.

**OUTGOING**—His brave and gregarious approach to life can be a total blast.

You might find a bull dog hard to live with because he's:

**ALL OR NOTHING**—A zero-to-sixty design can catch you off guard at times.

**POWERFUL**—His strength and force can overwhelm people and other animals.

**TOUCHY-FEELY**—If you value your personal space, he may get on your nerves (as well as your lap).

You might find yourself seeking professional help for:

- Destructive behavior, especially when left alone or unsupervised

- Incredible power and unmanageability/excitability on leash, especially around other animals

- Overenthusiastic behavior toward people—jumping, mouthing, roughhousing

- Protectiveness of one or more family members toward other people and animals

- Inflicting severe injuries on other animals in altercations due to strength (though not necessarily starting such altercations)

- General over-arousal in any number of high stimulation circumstances

## Family History

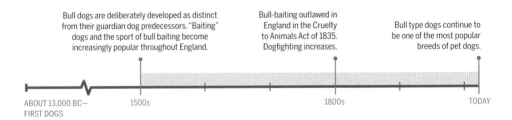

Bull dogs are deliberately developed as distinct from their guardian dog predecessors. "Baiting" dogs and the sport of bull baiting become increasingly popular throughout England.

Bull-baiting outlawed in England in the Cruelty to Animals Act of 1835. Dogfighting increases.

Bull type dogs continue to be one of the most popular breeds of pet dogs.

ABOUT 13,000 BC—
FIRST DOGS           1500s                    1800s                         TODAY

The bull dog type of dog is a genetic subgroup developed from the broad-mouthed mastiffs and the old British "pugnaces" ("attackers") guardian dogs.[49][50][51][52] Types of guardian dogs were used for thousands of years as courageous and impressive fighters in combat dating back to ancient Rome. They were prized as formidable gladiators. The popular blood-sport entertainment of the time would draw spectators by the thousands to

witness contests between men and between beasts.[54] Bears and other wild animals were often "baited"—chained and enraged—in an arena and then released to fight these powerful Molosser-type dogs in a contest of strength and skill.[53] The practice of animal baiting for entertainment and gambling shamefully continued as a common pastime for thousands of years, especially among the noble class and among royalty, with famous queens even breeding fighting dogs of their own for such events.[55]

By the sixteenth century, bears had become increasingly difficult to acquire, so bulls became the opponent of choice to compete against these dogs. So this group of dogs were developed specifically for the job of bringing down massive bulls. These "bull dogs" were largely developed from the smaller variety of their guardian ancestors—the "butcher's dog"—which had been used for herding, protecting the livestock, and for catching loose cattle.[56][57]

Predatory "gameness" and other distinct behavioral traits (such as having the ability to clench a bull by the nose and twist until the bull was brought down) were carefully bred into these dogs. Breeders wanted all of the dog's energy to be concentrated into a quick, full engagement of this *grab-bite* behavior, exaggerating this component of the dog's predatory sequence (*orient-eye-stalk-chase-grab bite-kill bite-dissect/consume*). They did not want a dog who was going to waste precious time and energy warning or hesitating to face his opponent. For the bull breeders, it was all about breeding a dog who could get the job done.

Remarkably, increasing the bull dog's ability to engage so formidably in altercations with other large target animals did not increase any tendencies for aggression toward people. In fact, bull dogs were deliberately bred for the ability to be easily handled. Contrary to popular opinion, these dogs were not bred to be more aggressive than other dogs but rather bred to be less aggressive and more docile in general nature (while perfecting their ability to unemotionally execute in a very specific set of circumstances).

Both bear and bull baiting were prevalent in other countries such as Spain, Portugal, Germany, and France; but England was by far the epicenter of the sport's activity.[58] Bull dogs were rapidly bred and improved throughout England as bull-baiting arenas became increasingly commonplace in townships until its peak in the early nineteenth century.[59][60][61] Bylaws requiring bulls to be baited before slaughter were even passed, as the meat was believed to be tenderized by the process of baiting.[62]

Bull-baiting and fighting between animals of any variety was eventually outlawed in England with the Cruelty to Animals Act of 1835. Unfortunately, this only set the stage for the underground emergence of dog fighting. The size of the arena required for dog fights—far smaller "pits" than those required for the baiting of larger animals—made it difficult for authorities to discover these illegal activities and enforce the law, and the sport flourished underground throughout Europe. By the end of the Civil War, interest and participation in dogfighting was widespread across the United States as well.

*The New Book of the Dog: A Comprehensive Natural History Of British Dogs And Their Foreign Relatives, With Chapters On Law, Breeding, Kennel Management, And Veterinary Treatment* (1907, Cassell).

Bull dogs of many varieties have been developed since the dawn of the world's first original bull-baiters bred in England. Though bull dogs are some of the most companionable pet dogs in the world, bred largely for their exceedingly good nature with people, bull dogs of many kinds have also continued to be selectively bred for their astonishing fighting attributes as the illegal world of dog fighting has continued to flourish into the twenty-first century.

Bull dogs have been used for other valuable jobs over the years, from defense against and the hunting of aggressive feral hogs to personal protection and companionship. They remain one of the most popular groups of dogs in the world, valued for their remarkable temperaments and adaptiveness to pet lifestyles outside of the contest environment.

## Upbringing

Parenting a bull dog puppy right means creating positive and constructive exposure to a wide range of people, animals, and circumstances. In particular, it is valuable for your bull dog to gain conflict resolution skills with other dogs of various ages and personalities. You would be wise to find some super-cool older dogs to teach your puppy the ropes about manners and the subtler forms of communication so he can learn that, when it comes to play and trouble, less is more. You can also help him to stop rough play before it escalates, with a quick break to cool off, if he gets too worked up.

Show him what he *can* do with all that might and courage. Provide large and durable toys and encourage him to wrestle them in order to target his natural full-body athleticism on something other than people and animals who might not find these kinds of games so much fun.

You really want your bull dog's natural lightheartedness to always take the lead in life, and you can do a great deal to help him approach events with the laid-back demeanor that is also part of his essential character. Fundamentally, you want to try to avoid the heat of the moment; so step in to help him take it down a notch when his engine really gets running during play or other activities. *Positive and mellow* should be the goal throughout socialization, and *good impulse control* the goal throughout early training in life. While that brain of his is still developing, play games like Red Light, Green Light, in order to teach him how to turn it all off at the drop of a hat. You want a puppy who has been there, done that and knows how to ride life in low gear without hitting top speed.

## Interests and Hobbies

He loves a good challenge. He is ambitious and is up for just about anything so long as it promises a good time. Using his profound physical strength in creative ways is usually at the top of the list for a bull dog; for instance: activities like couch hopping, toy shredding, rock climbing, tug-of-war, and rolling around with dog buddies. But then again so is spending the entire day laid out on top of your legs snoring in your king-sized bed. He is a magnificent contradiction at a glance—relentlessly entertaining in one moment and impossibly lazy in another.

He is surprisingly flexible and undemanding about what, exactly, it is that he needs on a day-to-day basis. A bull dog will make the most of any situation, and so makes an incredibly cooperative companion. It's all about going with the flow, living it up, rocking it out, and living each moment to the fullest.

He has a great attitude about acquiring new interests and trying new things, and will put his heart into just about any activity that seems like it will be a good time. Hide-and-seek the person, bobbing for bones in the bathtub, soccer one-on-one in the backyard, surfing the back seat with his head out the window on the way to the park, or a hike in the woods—these are almost definite wins with him. A bull dog just needs his partner to put him in the right kinds of situations, since he is inclined to go "all in." Even if he is a social butterfly and a dog park regular, a busy Saturday there could feel more like a mosh pit than a social event, and he might get a little carried away with the party vibe and crash the scene. The piñata you got for your weekend barbecue isn't likely to survive the first five minutes once he realizes that people are having a blast knocking the tar out of it—he will probably want to get in on that fun, and may take it a little too far. It is easy to enjoy almost anything with a bull dog, provided that you pick and choose activities he can engage in comfortably for all parties. If you aren't prepared for his enthusiasm, his outgoing approach may, indeed, come on too strong and accidentally wreak havoc in a moment.

## Education

The bull dog is an intelligent animal developed to live and work closely alongside people. His general MO is to comfortably go along with the instructor's directions—up to a point. For a bull dog, there is a clear moment at which

American Pit Bull Terrier

our instructions become secondary, at best. Once his adrenaline has fully kicked in, he can be impenetrably focused on the object of his engagement, and you may wonder if he remembers that you exist at all.

This isn't his fault, and it is largely not even a training or educational issue. Bull dogs were bred to be adrenaline junkies, and just like us they can get completely "in the zone" when they are doing their thing. Ignoring you in these moments is not deliberate; it's chemical. He gets hooked by his own DNA running the "Just do it!" software program. Your job, as his primary educator, will be to help him to stay away from this addiction in the first place.

Every time your bull dog goes *all out*, it is like a hit to his brain. He loves it. He wants more. As long as he is there, the whole world just melts away. And, once he is there, he is no longer making decisions or learning anything at all. The most important thing that you can do is to constantly manage his engine temperature so that he doesn't overheat into his adrenaline-junkie zone. Keep him cool by directing his attention to you every time life gets a little bit exciting. As long as he hasn't boiled over, he will be highly responsive to your handling. Work daily to condition a redirect to you under escalating moments of stimulation; be careful to have a plan in place to catch him before he loses sight of you altogether.

## Lifestyle

That bull dog of yours is going to boldly make himself at home just about anywhere. As long as he has had positive experiences and socialization, he should not be limited to any particular kind of environment. The most important consideration for life with your bull dog is simply to have good management practices wherever you are, so that you are controlling events that unfold (or having those tools in place to get control at a moment's notice).

HOME LIFE—All in all, your bull dog is going to make a great at-home companion and meet your expectations about indoor behavior far more easily than some of the hunting and working breeds will. He can be a couch-potato master cuddler with the best of them on a rainy day, and he can take a hint about leaving you alone when you are on deadline at your computer, and just go chew his bone.

But like many things with a bull dog, his household behavior may be all or nothing. He may go three weeks without chewing up a thing in your house while you are at work and then one day decide to take his frustrations out on your new leather sofa, set off when the neighbor's cat decided to sit right outside his favorite window. But don't dismay. Just take extra steps. Generally, these dogs are far better behaved indoors as pets than many other working breeds, content as they are to be "off" (passed out upside down on that leather sofa without a care in the world) as much as "on." Take him for a good long walk in the morning, then close the curtains, turn on the TV, and buy him a totally amazing bone to chew on and bury it at the bottom of his special toy basket you bring out only when you leave. Chances are you will find a perfect (albeit toy-covered) household when you return.

He may be a complete doll with all of your houseguests for hours on end during the dinner parties you have . . . after knocking your girlfriend clear off her feet as he gleefully pounced on her when she first arrived. Similarly, he and the cat may be best friends in your bed in the mornings, snuggling and sleeping peacefully for hours; but the cat knows better than to run through the house at top speed if the dog is up and moving, lest he find himself covered in drool after a well-meaning round of play. Not all bulls are going to have such raucous moments in the pursuit of fun, but it shouldn't be surprising if they do.

You can throw away your television for all of the entertainment you get from living with a bull dog, his antics and expressions amusing even in his sleep as he snores and contorts himself into ridiculous positions. His playtime can provide endless hours of laughter therapy for the entire family, as he creatively engages virtually any opportunity for fun. As long as he has plenty of appropriate toys and beds of his own to enjoy, your cherished belongings will most likely be safe from his clownish endeavors.

A bull dog coexists pleasantly with other humans and animals in the home, especially when simple steps are taken to ensure that levels of excitement or tension never get out of hand. He is not likely to *start* a fight, but if someone else picks one he is likely to answer strongly. Ensure that accidental contests do not arise between pets by feeding them separately, picking up food bowls when they're done, keeping high-value bones or toys put away, etc. Don't leave him alone with conditions that could potentially get him into high gear. Put precautions in place: baby gates, curtains, and background noise to wash out neighbors and kids on bikes outside. An ounce of prevention is worth its weight in gold. Maintaining a calm and well-managed, though fun, home environment will be ideal for him.

Even though he may look like he spends thirty hours a week in the gym for all the muscles he has, you may be surprised to find out that he is content with an urban lifestyle and leashed walks as daily exercise. He definitely needs his opportunities to stretch his legs and will benefit from routine activity, but he does not require a fenced yard or constant activity in order to be sane. He actually does really well as an inside dog. He does not, however, respond well to excessive confinement and will become frustrated by long periods of time in small quarters such as crates or on leashes. It is important that you have a plan in place to ensure that he does not spend too much time confined, and that he receives the periodic levels of exercise and stimulation he requires.

Most bull dogs are exceedingly friendly with strangers, but they do maintain the protective genes of their ancestral guardian predecessors. Practice the arousal level management when you have company in your home. Ensure that he observes that everything is cool and calm before he greets new people. This is best for everyone since many people are, in fact, quite fearful of bull dogs and yours will sense their discomfort (and could possibly misunderstand it) if your guests become overwhelmed by a powerful hello when they walk in your front door.

## HOME LIFE SCORE: 3 out of 5

SERIOUSLY CHALLENGING                                    THE EASY LIFE

Bull dogs would qualify for the highest rating in ease of home lifestyle if it were not for the 5 percent of the time that they make you want to give them the lowest possible score imaginable. They are easy-schmeezy all day long, and then a total handful. Just stay one step ahead of them by always having a master plan and an eye on the situation, and you will be totally fine.

**PUBLIC LIFE**—Be prepared and be happy. The right collar, the right leash, the right no-pull harness, the right moves—and you will be golden walking downtown or in the park with your bull dog. Tolerance, patience, and stoicism all come easy for him. But so does drama. Your job, walking through the world with him, is just to keep him out of it.

So, don't wing it with your bull dog. Enjoy peaceful, lovely strolls through the park. Have a head collar for your small horse to wear so that you have a grip in case he gets a little excited (he *is* stronger than you, after all). Work on redirecting him effectively when he gets interested in something *before* you lose him to the adrenaline zone, so all stays totally mellow.

Be mindful about how closely you pass other dogs, given how unruly many of them can be (and how unmanaged their behavior on the leash often is), so that you don't get caught off guard by someone else's lack of preparedness. For bull dogs, the "hold back" on leashes and presentation of another dog approaching can resemble a contest of sorts. Another "friendly" dog walking toward him with boundless "Here I come!" energy can set off your bull dog. Rather than misunderstanding your dog's unintentional reactions to these kinds of scenarios, simply recognize them and avoid them. Keep some distance, step aside, step between your dog and the excitement, and move along. Teach your bull dog that he can comfortably mind his own business and that you have the situation under control. Wing it—and you are likely to be flying through the air one fine day.

PUBLIC LIFE SCORE: 3 out of 5

PUBLIC EMBARRASSMENT                    SOCIAL BREEZE

There is an art to navigating through the world with this powerful
machine of a dog. If you master it, you will be happy on the road.

**PERSONAL LIFE**—You had better like PDA and grand displays of appreciation if you get involved with a bull dog. They are as all-in about you and your relationship as they are about everything else in life. You will feel at times as if you have acquired another appendage for all of the touching, leaning, and kissing going on. If you are naturally aloof and shy, get ready to break out of your comfort zone with your new BFF.

A bull dog's all-or-nothing mentality can be harnessed and facilitated. You can create a life of rainbows and unicorns for him and live on cloud nine together in complete bliss. He will buy in, sweetly and even naïvely, to the idea that life is totally perfect. He will want for nothing—content to be lighthearted and in the moment without a care. You can have an endearing and devoted partner with whom you enjoy a thousand adventures.

But this heart-on-his-sleeve guy can also get his feelings hurt, and may take things personally after a bad day. He is sensitive to experiences and may be very opinionated about the actions of others. If you get adversarial with him, or if there is an altercation between him and another human or animal family member, he can be hard pressed to let it go. He can be rather resistant to changing his mind when something has upset him, and quick to react emotionally if the scenario reminds him of a previous conflict. It is never advisable to get confrontational or physically corrective with any dog, in my opinion, but this is never truer than with a bull dog. Trust, patience, love, and thoughtful preparation will be the tools you need for this relationship.

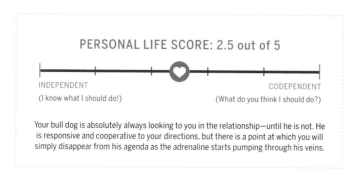

PERSONAL LIFE SCORE: 2.5 out of 5

INDEPENDENT
(I know what I should do!)

CODEPENDENT
(What do you think I should do?)

Your bull dog is absolutely always looking to you in the relationship—until he is not. He is responsive and cooperative to your directions, but there is a point at which you will simply disappear from his agenda as the adrenaline starts pumping through his veins.

## KEY CONCEPT: The Arousal-Aggression Continuum

Bull dogs get a bad (and mistaken) rap as vicious animals. As a matter of fact, this kind of dog is far less likely to get aggressive with people and other animals than many other breeds. Some of the little things that may irk more edgy dogs seem to simply roll off the backs of bull dogs like water. They are, therefore, one of the most enjoyable and friendly kinds of dogs in the world to live with.

So why the reputation? What about all of these reports about them "turning" and "flipping"? The truth is, bull dogs are pretty misunderstood on a practical level. Bull dogs need to be appreciated as simply *high-arousal* dogs genetically—rather than vicious—and handled accordingly.

What does that mean? *Arousal* in this case is a term referring to the electric system of the dog's body (the nervous system). In any animal, the system gets electrically "charged" by stimulation from the environment, with multiple significant events creating larger and more lasting charges in the body. As the charges build up or increase, the body starts to prepare itself for *fight or flight*. In nature, this is a highly adaptive—and genius—system for helping an animal survive those moments that demand a response of aggression or retreat.

In wild animals, the *arousal* level is constantly regulated in order to conserve vital energy that might be wasted gearing up for an unnecessary reaction. The animal is not easily aroused by unimportant events, and has mechanisms (such as "shaking it off") to physically release the charges as they occur in the body and so regulate the level of arousal in the nervous system. But humans have tinkered with this system by breeding dogs selectively for different behaviors. We made critical changes to the nervous systems of different kinds of dogs, desiring weaker responses to some things and stronger responses to others.

Bull dogs have been carefully selected for a uniquely delineated set of responses on a neurological level. The people who bred these dogs did not want them to waste energy reacting to the little things. A dog who idled very low for much of the time—far from hyperactive—was ideal. Ironically,

English Bull Dog

the *low-arousal* genetic stage of the guardian breeds was the perfect base for such a dog, willing as these protectors were to conserve their energy for the moment in which an action was required. When breeding for a bull dog, however, people still desired the conservation of energy but wanted a dog who could then engage more quickly to a very high level of arousal when the moment finally arrived. Breeders succeeded in creating just that: a *high-arousal* dog who could be easily moved from steady quietude into a suddenly charged "zone" (aggression).

To those on the outside of this neurological explanation, it may look like these dogs just unpredictably change into some "red zone" when, in fact, they are actually just high-arousal animals responding pretty predictably to an escalated circumstance and a heated atmosphere. It's not rocket science to stay out of trouble with a bull dog. As long as you keep it chill and copacetic, your bull dog can be cool as a cucumber all day long.

Just think of him as a high-horsepower race car. He has the potential to go zero-to-sixty at the drop of a hat, but he can also spend his entire life cruising around at thirty miles an hour. Your job is to keep him out of the race, prevent him from revving up at the starting line, and ensure that life isn't pressing the gas pedal and pushing him into top speed. You keep him in low gear by intervening when things get exciting and giving him a break for a few minutes to settle it all down. If he is too stimulated by a situation, go ahead and physically remove him before an altercation can occur so that he can return to a calmer state. Life happens, of course, and you may find that you are unable to prevent a high-arousal situation for your bull dog; so stack the deck by having effective collars (head halters are great for having control of his strength when he surges out toward a team of skateboarders) and interventions (quick-draw collar leashes can make it easy to get ahold of him before he gets ahold of one of the ducks in the lake). Whenever there is an atmosphere of excitement in the air, and when his blood starts pumping in response, you want to help him return to that low-gear mellow state, and then reward him well for his cooperation.

Bull Dog Relationship Survival Key:

- 🐾 Take steps to keep his system in its natural low gear so that his **GENETIC** high-arousal response to excitement doesn't get the better of him.

- 🐾 Ensure he has adequate opportunities to express himself, make sure he is very well-managed, and not overly confined in his daily **ENVIRONMENT**.

- 🐾 Keep that brain in **LEARNING** and thinking mode by regulating his excitement levels and impulses.

- 🐾 Relish his bigger-than-life personality for all that it is as you steer clear of trouble traps.

## MEET YOUR...

# Herding Dog

### "WORKING WINGMAN"

Australian Cattle Dog

Australian Shepherd

## TYPES OF HERDING DOGS

Australian Cattle Dog (Blue Heeler) · Australian Kelpie · Australian Shepherd · Bearded Collie ·
Beauceron · Belgian Groenendael · Belgian Malinois · Belgian Sheepdog · Belgian Tervuren ·
Berger Picard · Border Collie · Briard · Cardigan Welsh Corgi · German Shepherd · Old English
Sheepdog · Pembroke Welsh Corgi · Polish Lowland Sheepdog · Puli · Pumi · Pyrenean Sheepdog ·
Shetland Sheepdog · Standard Collie · Swedish Vallhund · mixes of any of the above breeds

### ♡ You'll fall in love with your herding dog because she's:

**A ROBIN TO YOUR BATMAN—**
Ready to heed the call for any
mission on the horizon, she
will not rest as long as there is
an adventure to be had.

**ATTENTIVE—**She is keenly
aware of her environment, as
well as her partner's emotions
and instructions.

**RESPONSIBLE—**This type-A
personality keeps her *i*'s dotted
and her *t*'s crossed with rules,
routines, work, and games.

### 💤 You might find a herding dog hard to live with because she's:

**BOSSY—**She is a regulator, here
to establish law and order by
managing the living room,
neighborhood, park, and
natural universe.

**A WORKAHOLIC—**Her mental
and physical ambition can
make her overwhelming and
exhausting at times, especially if
you have a quiet indoor lifestyle.

**CLINGY—**Her otherwise
adorable person-focus can be a
little on the unhealthy side.

You might find yourself seeking professional help for:

- Chasing fast-moving objects like cars, bikes, skateboards, joggers, cats, and children

- Controlling behavior toward other pets or family members possibly manifesting as threats or aggression

- Sensory hypersensitivity: to lights, shadows, sounds, and motion

- Excessive barking—at events, at her environment, and at people and animals

- Nipping the feet or legs of people and animals

- Protectiveness of territory and social members

- Threatening or aggressive behavior toward visitors

- Hyperactivity, agitation, or restless behavior

- Overexcitement, threatening or aggressive-appearing displays toward other animals, people, bikes, cars, etc.

- Neurotic, repetitive, and obsessive behaviors/OCD such as spinning, tail-chasing, retrieving, circling, and barking

## Family History

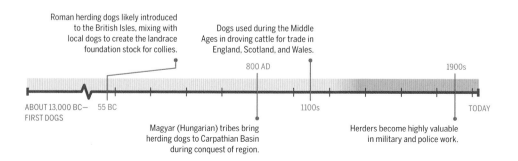

Roman herding dogs likely introduced to the British Isles, mixing with local dogs to create the landrace foundation stock for collies.

Dogs used during the Middle Ages in droving cattle for trade in England, Scotland, and Wales.

800 AD

1900s

ABOUT 13,000 BC—
FIRST DOGS

55 BC

1100s

TODAY

Magyar (Hungarian) tribes bring herding dogs to Carpathian Basin during conquest of region.

Herders become highly valuable in military and police work.

Once livestock was domesticated, humans required dogs to help them *protect* and *move* the large groups of animals so critical to their survival. Guardian dogs were among the first dogs in history to be employed for the task of defending, as early shepherds faced threats of animal (as well as human) predators in their pastures and trade routes. But the guardians, useful as they were, could fulfill only one of these two primary niches well. They were deliberately developed to *not* chase the animals they protected, and so were limited in their ability to help when it came to the job of *moving* them; they were not supposed to have the instincts to startle, stalk, or agitate the flocks and herds. As migration and trade expanded across Eurasia, shepherds increasingly needed to be able to efficiently motivate and organize their animals. They would need another kind of dog altogether to do that—a hunter of sorts—to give chase.

So it's no surprise that some of the first dogs used for herding animals were those early natural dogs with intact predatory instincts to stalk, pursue, and corner prey. Many of the primitive medium-sized Asian and northern Spitz breeds of dogs are thought to have occasionally been used for "coarse herding" (chasing, barking at, moving, or holding herd animals without attacking them) in addition to their primary roles of protecting and hunting.[63][64]

Like many of the more modern breeds, the fruits of our labor were largely the result of trial and error. It was no small task trying to create a dog that would have a high predatory instinct to stalk and rush after moving animals without actually hurting them (it would be pretty counterproductive to a shepherd to have his own dog kill his sheep). Not to mention that we needed a dog who was athletic and hardy enough to work ridiculously long hours in harsh terrain and be responsive enough to human directions to move the animals where we needed them to go (as opposed to running aimless circles around them).

People also modified herding dogs into sub-experts within this group, selecting them for the different kinds of animals we needed help moving and the circumstances in which we needed to move them. Some dogs were used to simply drive herds from one location to another, while others were used to more closely organize a flock. Slightly less assertive dogs were needed for working with sensitive sheep; more aggressive dogs were required for motivating more imposing cattle. Certain dogs were used for holding the animals back with a fixed stare at the right distance, and others were employed for chasing or retrieving animals with quick movements.

Not surprisingly, herding behaviors have also proved to be very useful in military and police capacities in more recent years. The dogs' responsiveness to their handler, propensity for intense barking, acute perceptiveness to changes in their environment, reactivity to movement, and strong drive to work have made them proficient human herders. A number of breeds have been bred so specifically for these roles that they have even become genetically distinct from other herding breeds. From border patrol to crowd control, dogs such as the German and Belgian Shepherds have become world renowned for their astonishing aptitude at these modern specialties.

Herding dogs are undeniably one of the most dynamic groups of dogs, capable of working closely alongside their partner in a variety of highly demanding conditions. The challenge in living with one in the twenty-first century, should you find yourself in such a relationship, is not so much how to get her on board but rather how to get her to relax and take it easy in a pet lifestyle. She was designed to work an eighteen-hour day on the farm. It's against her very nature to put her feet up and kick back.

## Upbringing

Your herding dog was bred to not miss anything. She is taking notes all the time (and cross-referencing them with other notes in order to analyze and predict possibilities for the future). Factor in the critical period's predisposal for sensitive learning and absorption of new information, and you

*The Dog Book: A Popular History of the Dog, with Practical Information as to Care and Management of House, Kennel, and Exhibition Dogs; And Descriptions of All the Important Breeds* (1906, Doubleday).

have one heck of an opportunity to make certain impressions on her when she is young. You also have plenty of chances to accidentally set the stage for complete disasters later in life, if you aren't paying close attention. Do your best to be a capable and engaging sheriff to your overzealous deputy from the jump. Be one step ahead and mentally prepared to step up and take the reins at all times.

Whatever you do, remember that your puppy is bred to *work*. All the time. At your side. Doing anything that needs to be done. If you are not aware of this, or if you are not engaging her potential, she will undoubtedly write her own job description and forge missions of her own. You have just brought home a full-time ambitious wingman, assistant, and helper. Explain *everything* about the life you plan to share with her; you're training a rookie here. She will eagerly take your lead—*if* you constantly provide it.

Dogs bred for centuries to follow extremely subtle nuances of voice, tone, sounds, language, and movement in order to move flocks of animals with precision have developed an intrinsic attention to the details of our behavior, and to the information and directions we provide—including what we are actually saying. While they do not comprehend the meanings our words in the exact manner that humans do, they learn to associate certain patterns of sounds with other events in their environment, and thus glean our expectations and intentions. Just as young children learn to make sense of their world and the rules as we explain it all to them, dogs can, similarly, put the pieces together as we go through the world with them. Herding dogs, more than any other group, are widely known for their receptive language ability—likely because we bred them to closely follow human directions in the complex process of herding animals. Not only is she *capable* of understanding more words than you can imagine; she *needs* you to provide them. Talk to her, constantly. Let people stare.

So, get on the ball and show her the ropes: Okay, puppy, here's the deal. We live in the twenty-first century. There are no sheep in Boston. We live in a small suburban house where friendly, treat-bearing people come over and visit for social occasions. They are not sheep, or intruders. I will handle things; you're on lunch break. There are other dogs, cats, and people living in our neighborhood who will regularly appear outside your fence and windows. They are not sheep, or intruders. Stand down and quietly supervise from a distance, stakeout style. Good work. When we go out into the field together, I will explain all of the details to you as we go along. At no point will you need to treat any fast-moving wheeled and legged objects as sheep, or intruders. I will let you know if any action is required of you. Stand by for your instructions, waiting in vigil at my side, as you so do so well. Nice job. Have a cookie.

On walks we politely mind our own business and, when necessary, socialize graciously. On restaurant patios we lie down under the table and remain quiet as to not disturb other diners or the staff—you are undercover, incognito. Well done. At the vet we tolerate rude invasions of personal space for a health screening. Sorry, mandatory. Bonus treats for camaraderie and patience with the staff. Don't be bossy with your fellow officers at the park. They don't like it. When we hit the trailhead, remain calm and composed as we count down to the start of the daily mission to locate the lost ghost sheep in the woods. *5, 4, 3, 2, 1. Go!*

Get ready. This herding dog, even as a baby, will make your life pretty exciting. Cute and innocent-looking as she is at eight weeks, this pup is not for the lazy, uncreative, or faint of heart.

## Interests and Hobbies

Work, work, work. Breed a dog for hundreds of years to function proficiently and even occasionally multitask, and you get a little bit of neuroticism about over-functioning in life. For her, idle paws are indeed the devil's play things. Passivity is just not in her vocabulary. For her, work is fun. Work is life. Unemployment is misery.

She is not picky about the *kind* of work she does, as long as it is interesting. The more complex the task, the better. She definitely has her preferences for chasing anything that moves quickly, regulating anything out of

Shetland Sheepdog/Pembroke Welsh Corgi mix

the ordinary, or barking sharply and running circles around disorganized groups of people or animals. But she is quite flexible in her abilities, and surprisingly open to suggestions about redirecting her efforts elsewhere. You just have to write a clear job description for her.

Letting you know the alarm clock went off, bringing you the leash and your shoes, and keeping the cats off of the counters—these can all be part of her job. Barking every time a neighbor closes a car door, herding Grandpa to the bathroom, and protecting the family from the pizza man—not so much. You write her duties clearly through your feedback, moment to moment. Quite literally, what you feed into with encouragement, rewards, or energy will be perceived as part of the plan. What you unambiguously interrupt with quiet and pragmatic assertiveness—"That's absurd, you silly dog, sit down and mind your business, please"—will be recognized as erroneous. You have to be consistent, of course. And demonstrate that you are capable of getting control of any situation more efficiently than she. You have to fill the captain's shoes so she doesn't step up to the plate.

When it comes to satisfying a herding dog's interests, the focus and the burden rest squarely on your shoulders. Without your direction, provisions of meaningful tasks, and enthusiasm, she will be entirely lost. This workaholic hungers for a sense of accomplishment and a supervisor. She has the perception that she can make the world right and return order to the universe by your side. Let your imagination fill her cup with important assignments, high demands, and thrilling endeavors. Never stop teaching her new things, adding to her list of critical responsibilities as the little worker bee she is.

## Education

While she in no way lacks the motivation to pursue her own studies, she is definitely the type of student who will become anxious without a great deal of direction from her professor. She is a naturally poised apprentice who has been selected to look to you for information, to seek your constant instruction, and to garner your approval.

You will have no trouble whatsoever teaching her things. She will pick up new skills at the drop of a hat. You are more likely to underestimate her and not move quickly enough through the material than to be disappointed in her progress. She needs you to keep the bar high, and to continue to raise it, in order to stay engaged. This highly gifted student of yours can become problematic, and even anxious, if she is not properly challenged and led.

But on the other hand, you also need to be aware of her tipping point. Dogs bred to be such highly ambitious, hardworking, and intense animals can easily become "addicted" to their "work"; whether it is retrieving a ball or herding those sheep. Herding dogs can and do frequently get stuck repeating their favorite behavior, engaging in a type of obsessive-compulsive pattern that can be disruptive and unhealthy. Their obsession with their occupation can be so intense that they become dysfunctional, literally unable to think of anything other than their job, and anxiously awaiting their next opportunity to do it. It is indeed a bit tricky to balance the necessary satisfaction of your dog's instincts with the deliberate regulation of her obsession, but it is important to keep this in mind. She will need your help with regulation—requiring frequent breaks when "working," interruptions of "work" when it becomes escalated or cyclical, and praise for simply chilling out and doing something else.

She is the perpetual sponge, soaking up every detail in the world around her and attending to each nuance of your voice, emotions, demeanor, and cues. She needs you to give her clear, reliable verbal and behavioral information. In the same manner that a parent constantly explains the world and its meanings to a young child, a herding dog's teacher must realize that each moment is a lesson for their eager student. You explain, "We are in public. You need to mind your manners. Lie down and wait quietly while I have my coffee." As you do this, make sure you exhibit very different physical gestures from those you exhibited at home a few hours ago when you were wrestling on the floor with her.

Be consistent about the things that you say, the things that you do, and the way that you do them. Create patterns and protocols, and stick to them. Remember you are always a teacher—she is always watching, listening, and learning at your hand. You are responsible for the lessons, and school is never out.

Border Collie

## Lifestyle

Life with your herding dog can be beyond your wildest dreams, the very stuff the old *Lassie* episodes were made of. She has more capacity for communication, relationship, sport, fun, and work than almost any other kind of dog. The flip side is, you will really have to work for it. She is a fish out of water as a pet in the modern age, to say the least. If she is not adequately stimulated and challenged, she will suffer psychologically and become frustrated, neurotic, or even aggressive. If you go the necessary lengths to ensure her mental and behavioral health, however, you will be a partner to one incredible dog.

**HOME LIFE**—She will learn all of the rules of your home with ease. You will be bragging to your friends about the twenty-four hours it took to housebreak her and the four tricks she learned in the first week. She will figure out your daily patterns and work hard to accommodate them. She will be working so darn hard, as a matter of fact, that you may just lose your mind.

If you like to be left alone, this kind of dog may not be ideal for you. Like an overenthusiastic Girl Scout just dying to find out what the day has in store, she will merrily follow you around from room to room, watching your every move. It can get a little annoying. Or it can be absolutely wonderful.

You can tell her all about your friend Mary who is coming over in a minute and she will hang on your every word, too, cocking her head adorably. But unless you want to bring crime show drama right to your living room, you may want to remember to think ahead and lock the door. Mary may have been letting herself in without knocking for the past three years, but now that you have adopted a herding dog, she is likely to be perceived as an intruder by breaching protocol about the entrance of visitors into the home.

Create and follow a well-managed routine for visitors, as with everything else, and she'll be just fine. If you find she has a hard time conceding to your advice about company, you can also use a well-placed tether on the far side of your family room as an off-duty location. When someone comes knocking, she can be "clocked out" with an amazing bone away from the door for a few minutes as the person comes in and the dust settles. By taking control of events predictably, you will help your type-A dog relax. You never want to just wing it with your wingman.

In terms of your home life, give her plenty of information and instructions. Be diligent and patient as she reacts to the sights and sounds around your home. A herding dog will very likely bark, chase, or nip from time to time. Be aware that innocent nerf war games, spontaneous tickling fights, and romantic dances (and the other stuff that comes with those dances) can all be perceived as out of order and unacceptable to your little assistant manager.

Above all else, you will want to remember that your herding dog is simply not meant to spend a great deal of time confined, alone, indoors. Your natural worker simply will not fare well with your long days at work or indoor inactivity as a general rule. She will quickly develop neurotic and obsessive behaviors, unfit to adapt to the conditions of the average American pet. In order to avoid both of you going crazy in the confines of the home, you will need to find ways to work her body and mind. Start with plenty of difficult puzzle toys, herding balls, and exciting lessons in the indoor classroom. Give her a life filled with missions that push her to reach her great potential.

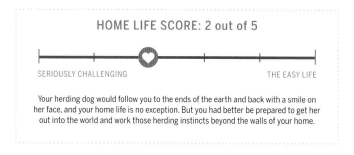

### HOME LIFE SCORE: 2 out of 5

SERIOUSLY CHALLENGING      THE EASY LIFE

Your herding dog would follow you to the ends of the earth and back with a smile on her face, and your home life is no exception. But you had better be prepared to get her out into the world and work those herding instincts beyond the walls of your home.

**PUBLIC LIFE**—While some herding dogs can be very outgoing when socialized extensively, many prefer to keep a more discerning social circle of people and other dogs. They are uniquely focused on their primary people and their family, and naturally concerned with order and boundaries. While going out into the world—into public life and its many adventures—is exactly what she needs to be sane, it can also present an awkward challenge at just about every turn.

Law and order. That's her MO. The person who reaches out uninvited to pet her, the truck making an enormous racket passing by, the rambunctious puppy jumping out to greet her, the schoolchildren running down the street—can all be perceived as violations warranting a swift correction by your four-legged officer. You will have to be the ever-mindful sheriff on the beat when you go out with her, providing clear directives at all times.

Her (and therefore your) experiences when you're out together have a great deal to do with the quality of communication and understanding between you. If she can trust that you are on the ball and you let her know how to handle things, you can just enjoy the day. Don't let the invasive petter and impulsive puppy reach her. Step away from the loud truck and posse of kids and ask her to sit and wait quietly as they pass. What concern of yours are they? You have better things to do. You are grooving to the *Mission Impossible* theme song in your head as you forge on toward the river, where you'll enjoy a game of "save the stick" together and a two-hour evening hike to find all those invisible sheep.

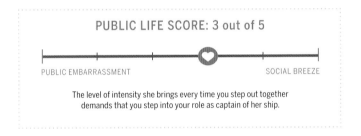

PUBLIC LIFE SCORE: 3 out of 5

PUBLIC EMBARRASSMENT                    SOCIAL BREEZE

The level of intensity she brings every time you step out together demands that you step into your role as captain of her ship.

**PERSONAL LIFE**—Being in a relationship with a herding dog is like having any high-maintenance, super-ambitious partner. You will find yourself as ridiculously impressed with her commitment and generosity of spirit with you as you are exhausted by her intensity about the partnership. Getting along has a lot to do with embracing her for who she is—recognizing that she may not be capable of just going with the flow or hanging out at times. Rather than letting yourself get exasperated, you can adopt a perspective of valuing all that she has to offer. This kind of dog needs constant attention and may cramp your independent style at times. There's no doubt that she's demanding of your time and energy. But she will give back to you what you give to her in spades. She may be exceptionally needy, but she is also made to respond to your every need.

It can feel a little ironic. A dog that is able to read your every thought and emotion so intuitively should not need you to define every aspect of life for her. But she does. She was not intended to make her own decisions or to self-entertain. The attributes that made her the responsive full-time working dog on a farm, closely attending to her shepherd, have put her at a great disadvantage in other regards. She is hyper-dependent on you, not just for your company and physical attention, but for her very sense of security about the world around her.

The once ideal companion of mankind finds herself in a frustrating predicament. Very few of us have lifestyles that allow us to take our dogs with us most of the time, and yet this is exactly what she needs to be in her true element. To be working alongside you—that is her place. It can honestly be a bit heart-wrenching to realize how utterly confused she is that she is unable to do so day after day.

If you can create some regular healthy outlets for her overachieving behavioral needs, and if you can tolerate a dog so creepily well-tuned to you that she reflects your every mood and manner, you will discover possibilities in a relationship with a herding dog unlike any you have ever experienced. Every bit of energy you put into the partnership, you will reap ten times over. You will be exhausted, and satisfied, by this kind of relationship. And so will your herding companion.

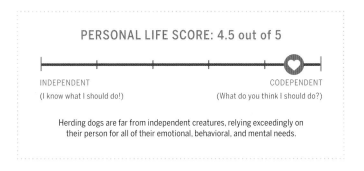

PERSONAL LIFE SCORE: 4.5 out of 5

INDEPENDENT
(I know what I should do!)

CODEPENDENT
(What do you think I should do?)

Herding dogs are far from independent creatures, relying exceedingly on their person for all of their emotional, behavioral, and mental needs.

## KEY CONCEPT: Sudden Environmental Contrasts

All animals learn about their world by finding patterns in the events around them. This enables them to recognize larger patterns of "normal" in their environments as well as situational patterns. By knowing the patterns—the sights, sounds, smells, and experiences of a place or context—one can more quickly distinguish the uncharacteristic events that pose unique threats and opportunities.

Herding dogs not only notice these distinct Sudden Environmental Contrasts (SEC's); they *specialize* in perceiving them and responding to them. Exaggerated by artificial selection in herders, this naturally adaptive phenomenon was exceedingly useful to humans. The ability to quickly recognize patterns and reflexively attend and respond to breaches had its place for a dog tasked with keeping head count, order, and safety in a large herd.

Organizing, moving, and protecting a group of animals requires constant attention to detail, anticipation of the behavior of others, and lightning-fast reflexes for responding to the moment's demands. Hypersensitivity to infractions against a rule is valuable in a herding dog helping a shepherd move a flock to a nearby pasture. But in a canine companion, it can be maddening.

One moment she is walking beautifully beside you as you stroll down the quiet street in the cool morning air; and the next you're struggling to hold the leash as she leaps and barks furiously at a man coming over the top of the hill. You cannot figure out how this same dog attended a downtown festival with you yesterday without incident, surrounded by masses of people from all walks of life.

Here's the reason: It's all about the contrast. Yesterday, you got out of your car on a busy street filled with people moving about, and your dog quickly perceived and adapted to the status quo of the scene. No one person or event stood out within the pattern to her, so she did not react. This morning, however, she observed a completely different picture, one without any people or animals moving about. Until he appeared. He violated the pattern.

Rather than pulling your hair out in exasperation over her remarkable sensitivity and reactivity to these kinds of events, develop an awareness of them yourself, and direct her accordingly. Once you start to perceive the world through her eyes a little better, you can be prepared to guide her rather than despair at her little outbursts.

Herding Dog Relationship Survival Key:

- 🐾 Prepare yourself for her herding **GENETICS** to micromanage the natural world.

- 🐾 Offer a structured and suspenseful **ENVIRONMENT** that satisfies her instincts for work.

- 🐾 Fulfill her almost supernatural propensity for complex **LEARNING** by endlessly finding new things for her to do (like fetching the remote, cleaning up her toys, getting you the leash, or finding your misplaced keys).

- 🐾 Recognize and embrace the awesome intensity of having a full-time canine wingman at your side.

# World Dog

## "RENAISSANCE DOG"

Mixed breed

Mixed breed

## TYPES OF WORLD DOGS

World dogs are not breeds created by humans with closed gene
pools or artificially selected jobs. Nature is the breeder in this case,
and has continued to create these dogs all over the world. Their
physical forms indicate that they have no specific predominant job
in their ancestry, other than to be good at simply being a dog.

**♥ You'll fall in love with your world dog because she's:**

**FLEXIBLE**—Adaptive to change, she goes with the flow, and is at home in many environments.

**PRACTICAL**—She is observant, self-sufficient, undemanding, low-maintenance, and efficient.

**GOOD-NATURED**—This dog is tolerant, solicitous, cooperative, docile, and level-headed.

**You might find a world dog hard to live with because she's:**

**AN OPPORTUNIST**—She's a trash-scavenging and poop-eating machine, her essence being that of the original opportunistic dog looking for leftovers of any kind.

**GOT YOUR NUMBER**—Your world dog is a human behavior expert who is reading and watching your every move.

**SELF-SERVING**—Her agenda and interest is her "job;" working for you is not.

You might find yourself seeking professional help for:

Any number of common dog behaviors that can get on your nerves—

🐾 peeing in the house

🐾 chewing on things that don't belong to her

🐾 getting on your furniture

🐾 barking at the neighbors' cats

🐾 stealing sandwiches off the coffee table

🐾 jumping on people

🐾 pulling on the leash

🐾 having her own agenda that may or may not involve following your directions

The earliest dogs of the world naturally evolve in ever-closer proximity to man, benefitting from their leftover resources

Genetically unmanaged by humans, free-roaming world dogs proliferate as independent opportunists in villages and cities around the globe while landrace breeds develop and contribute to their world dog gene pools.

World dogs occasionally interbreed with the newly emerging "purebred" modern dogs fashioned through Victorian breeding programs, with world dogs now labeled "mutts" and "mongrels" of low class heritage.

Autonomous, unregulated breedings continue to produce the "fittest" animals for their conditions, maintaining better overall health through genetic diversity and adaptivity to changing environments.

ABOUT 13,000 BC— FIRST DOGS    1000 AD    1400s    1900s    TODAY

## The #1 Dog on Earth

Roughly 80 percent of the dogs on the planet are not purebreds at all. Despite their unfettered breeding, they are the most popular, successful dogs on earth. And for a very good reason. Those very dogs in which we can identify absolutely no evidence of any particular breeding are in fact the most highly adaptive dogs of all. While humans have been busy creating dogs they desired for a particular purpose over the millennia, nature has

continued to do what it does best—designing animals that are simply well-suited to the world around them. We call them mutts, mongrels, and Heinz 57s. But they are, in fact, the *world dog*.

One great shift in perspective reveals that these dogs are a masterpiece of evolution—a modern reflection of the original evolutionary love story between humans and dogs. The purpose for these animals is to peacefully and successfully live alongside humans as they go about their lives in the twenty-first century. Across the globe, such a dog is always in the picture where people are found. They are often ignored and dismissed as we continue to prize the notion of pure-blooded animals. But they are, in actuality, natural perfection. Nature's intelligence, selecting for suitability to circumstances, is their respectable breeder. They are more likely to thrive in the niche of being our pets as a result. While many purebred dogs struggle to adjust to modern environments bearing little resemblance to the conditions for which they were bred, *world dogs* are able to continue to adapt to our changing conditions on their own. With no particular requirements for upbringing and education, hobbies, or lifestyle, the world dog is a remarkably compatible and enjoyable companion for many of us.

"Scene in the Principal Square of Trebizond," *Harper's Weekly*, 1896.

## HOME LIFE SCORE: 4 out of 5

SERIOUSLY CHALLENGING                    THE EASY LIFE

Amenable to all kinds of habitats, the world dog's pragmatic approach makes him flexible to a greater range of home life provisions than many dogs developed for more specific conditions and behaviors.

## PUBLIC LIFE SCORE: 4 out of 5

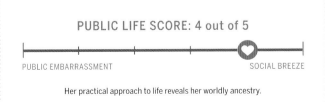

PUBLIC EMBARRASSMENT                    SOCIAL BREEZE

Her practical approach to life reveals her worldly ancestry.

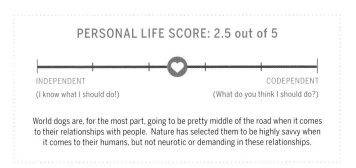

PERSONAL LIFE SCORE: 2.5 out of 5

INDEPENDENT                                    CODEPENDENT
(I know what I should do!)          (What do you think I should do?)

World dogs are, for the most part, going to be pretty middle of the road when it comes
to their relationships with people. Nature has selected them to be highly savvy when
it comes to their humans, but not neurotic or demanding in these relationships.

## KEY CONCEPT: Choice

Lying scattered around the town square in shaded doorways and across the long stretch of summer grass in the public park in Chacabuco, Argentina, a number of dogs are resting contentedly and surveying the traffic of men about them. They neither approach nor avoid the people walking by or sitting at cafés, but observe the happenings around them with subtle constant interest, interacting as nonchalantly and warmly with each other as the people do in this small Argentine town.

Fascinated, I wander around this park outside of my hotel and observe them, talk to them, invite them to interact with me. Though hard-pressed and far from rushed to disturb a good nap in the shade, they stretch their legs and approach with a reasonable scrutiny about my intentions, reading me for indications of opportunity or trouble. I am struck by their pragmatic confidence, their calm and friendly unobtrusive demeanor, as they lower their heads and lean into me for a scratch before taking interest in something or someone else across the street. They are not ill-behaved or invasive, but cautiously well-mannered and kind. They are as flea-bitten, fat, and happy a bunch of dogs as I have ever seen.

A woman has taken on a few of these creatures and formed a daily ritual with them that echoes the original common niche of the world's original dog over the continents and centuries. She has leftovers to spare, and the dogs are positioned there to scavenge them. When the right person appears from a certain door at a specific time in the afternoon, a dozen of these Chacabuco dogs are poised in waiting to move in on the café scraps of trimmed fat and last night's empanadas, which she carries out into the park. The dogs greet her with wagging tails and whimpers when she appears, following her closely toward a large tree where she empties the contents of a bag. They have taken all the right notes about the details of the events that occur in a certain place and time in their environment and respond accordingly.

If we go back a hundred years or more or travel outside of modern Western civilization, we will see the dog in this world environment as he has lived for thousands of years. We will see dogs living in very different ways than they do in our homes today. Dogs, since the dawn of human civilization and still throughout much of the undeveloped world, have lived among people not as pets as much as domesticated wildlife of sorts with loose alliances and arrangements with their human counterparts.

The quintessential dog of the world meanders freely through those village streets, looking for his best chances to eat a good meal and successfully reproduce. He follows his instincts to scavenge, hunt, mate, and socialize to the benefit of his own interests and the survival of his genes. Dog as he is, he is astutely aware of and keen to capitalize on the behavior of humans, valuable resource jackpots that they are for dogs with their wasteful disposal of delicious leftovers.

This animal fits well within his many daily changing environmental conditions and parts for him to play—cute begging "poor dog" for the Western tourists, competitive trash marauder among other dogs, agile traffic dodger—because he developed within and because of these conditions. He is right where he belongs, where nature has designed him to be. He is right at home, this dog of the world. We Westerners often want to "rescue" him from these circumstances, though he might not need rescuing at all.

Even when his cards are down, the village dog enjoys a richness of experience that many captive animals do not. Life may not always be easy for him, but his L.E.G.S.®—his learning, his environment, his genetics,

Mixed breed

and his self—work well together in harmony and balance. He has what so many of our beloved dogs have largely lost, as they have been taken in and granted the many luxuries that we provide as our pets: control over his own choices. He has the autonomy to engage all four of his L.E.G.S. in balance with each other, employing his genes to his environment as he continues to learn how to make the best of his unique journey on earth.

Our pet dog does not have the same options or opportunities. Leash laws, pet owner liability, and our personal commitment to our companion's well-being dictates that we make many choices for him. Left to his own

Mixed breed

devices in any American city, a pet dog will almost surely find himself in great trouble or danger in short order. He lacks the skills to hack it without our guidance. That's the deal, right or wrong. We are in the precarious and profoundly important position of walking a very thin line for him, then, if we are to offer any semblance of balance to our canine friends.

We must recognize his need to have control over his own choices whenever possible, giving him as many appropriate chances to express himself naturally without constraints as we can—in the woods, in the yard, at the lake, on the beach, and in our homes. At the same time, we must never forget our role as his captain. We sail on a certain ship together in this modern pet relationship—one built of fences, leashes, and walls—that he will never be able to sail on his own.

So let's try to acknowledge the drive our dogs have for a little taste of freedom—whether they are world dogs of mixed heritage or pure breeds. We have a responsibility to let our pets make their own choices when we can. Let's let them decide whether to come in or go out, to go over or under, to get on or get off, to come now or come later, to approach or to leave, to be touched or not, to play or to sleep. They are indeed captive animals as our pets, even if they are spoiled rotten; but they don't have to be prisoners.

World Dog Relationship Survival Key:

- 🐾 Recognize that she's going to **LEARN** what things mean *for her*, what works *for her*, and act accordingly.

- 🐾 Enjoy her adaptability to different **ENVIRONMENTS** and socialize her to their elements.

- 🐾 Remember that she is a **GENETIC** freeloader and embrace her innocently selfish ways.

- 🐾 Know that she is one in a million, and your relationship with her is completely unique.

# Self

He is one in a million. There is no other dog on the planet exactly like him. He is an individual with his own story and his own personality, living in a body only he can inhabit. He is Bob.

You brought Bob home from the shelter a year ago, eight years old and mostly deaf. He has a limp in his rear left leg from a break that never quite healed right, and the arthritis to go along with it. You were not looking for an older dog. But he met all of your requirements for a companion, and you and Bob just hit it off.

Bob's environment, his learning habits, and his genetics all play a huge role in his behavior, as you now know. But there's one last piece of the puzzle: the self. The self is the umbrella that contains all the aspects of your dog that are unique to him. A dog's sex, particular hormonal makeup, his age, his health, and his life experiences are all part of what makes him one of a kind. These factors can have profound effects on how he behaves throughout the course of his lifetime. Disabilities, his diet, or illness may change his perceptions, his moods, and his habits. Whether he is feeling the blinding thrill of testosterone hitting his system for the first time as an adolescent male or the edgy defensiveness of a vulnerable elder dog compromised by his declining functions, your dog is subject to these influences.

You love to tell all of your friends about Bob. For the first month you had him, he had to wear the cone of shame because he wouldn't leave his stitches alone after his neuter. He bumped into everything, and you laughed harder than you had in years, as he merrily brought you that little green ball time and again, no matter how long it took him to manage to scoop it up with that thing on his head. That ball might as well have been made of gold for how important it was to him. He was uninterested in dropping it even for his gourmet meals. You wouldn't have thought he was underweight back then for how stinking snobby he was about his food, turning his nose up at everything but the highest-quality home-cooked chicken dinners. All of these nuances that make Bob and his story unique are a critical aspect of the self. Just like we are, dogs are individuals.

You look down at your adorable, incorrigible, perfectly irreplaceable friend Bob who has somehow trained you to feed him better than you do yourself *and* to allow a dog in your bed after you swore you would never share it with a furry pet again. You kiss his fuzzy chicken breath dog face as he curls up next to your pillow. You love the little stinker more than anything. He is *your* dog. He is Bob.

You experience him so intimately, so remarkably, every day. In many ways you may feel closer to him than to many people in your life. And yet, a large part of Bob's internal world is still impossible for you to understand completely. You can make some educated guesses about Bob's inner life based on what you can see of his outer life. You know how old he is by the plaque on his teeth. You can assume his male hormones have decreased because he is missing his family jewels. You can determine he doesn't hear very well because when you broke a glass bowl six feet from where he was sleeping, his ears didn't even twitch. These are the kinds of facts you are given about a dog when you adopt him, and the kind of descriptions we use to make assumptions about how our dog is feeling and what he might be thinking.

What you experience with your dog—whether he is snapping at you when you roll over on him in the middle of the night, or he's urinating on the rug just minutes after you took him outside—can sometimes be explained by a unique factor of his internal self. His rear leg is painful and he snapped at you because it hurt when you bumped it. He peed on the floor because he has a urinary tract infection.

When considering the possibility that the self is behind the wheel of your dog's behavior, think about the big six. Examine the following: Age (development and condition related to age), Sex (M/F and Fixed/Intact), Health (disease, infection, virus, parasite), Nutrition (quality, quantity, and tolerance/allergy), Disability (deafness, blindness, amputation, etc.), and Individual (the wild-card factor).

## ♥ Age

**FEAR PERIODS.** There are two primary developmental fear periods in puppies that can make your canine kid act like he's suddenly seeing ghosts, now afraid of things in his environment that rolled off him days before. While they vary a bit from individual to individual, the first fear period is generally from eight to eleven weeks of age, and the second from six to fourteen months. These phases can seem to be minimal and last just a few short days, or they can feel like they drag on for months. Try to be confidently assuring yet sensitive to not push your puppy into overwhelming or stressful experiences during this time.

**ADOLESCENCE.** Teenage dogs can be as unbelievably difficult and frustrating to live with as human teens. During this developmental period (roughly six to eighteen months), your sweet little puppy is gradually becoming a young adult. The hormones hit, blinding all logic. Exciting new urges to roam and sniff and pee on things arise. Decision making, judgment, and impulse control go out the window, while risk taking and impulsivity skyrocket. People may feel their dog has forgotten everything they'd ever taught them during this time, and even wonder if their little beast has gone quite mad (in fact, this is the age when most dogs are surrendered to animal shelters). Be patient, be consistent, and know that it is all just a normal part of development that your dog needs you to ride out with confidence.

### ♥ Sex

**PHEROMONES.** Intact males and females can present a catalyst for social tensions, conflict, and altercations between dogs—even when the intact animal has nothing to do with it. When a dog's brain is dominated by the olfactory cortex (smell)—either the "scent of a woman" or the alluring stud factor of intact animals—it can pique more than the interest of other dogs. Reproduction is one of nature's most fundamental resources, and these signals can set off a host of challenges both inside a home and in neutral environments. Be aware of the possibility that the introduction of a sexually intact animal can strike a match in any given social scene between otherwise harmonious companions.

### ♥ Health

**PAIN.** Dogs hide pain way better than we do. Many owners are surprised to discover, after a visit to their veterinarian or an experienced behavior specialist, that their dog has been in pain for some time. An abscessed tooth, a bad hip, an ear infection, or even a disease such as cancer could be taking a serious toll on your buddy, and you wouldn't even know it. Changes in behavior are sometimes the only cue that our dog is in trouble; that's why it is so important to consider that health issues could be a possible explanation for strange behavior.

**AGGRESSION AND ILLNESS.** A healthy dog can, on rare occasions, behave aggressively toward an unhealthy dog in the home—even if the animals have been close companions for years. The symptoms, smells, and behaviors associated with disease in the unhealthy dog may act as instinctive signals to the other dog, triggering an attack on the weaker animal. Though this does not occur often, it is important not to blame the aggressor unfairly or to make assumptions about the dog's intentions and temperament if such an event should occur.

### ♥ Nutrition

**DIET.** "You are what you eat" doesn't just apply to people. Dogs' bodies are significantly affected by what they consume, and particularly if they are not consuming enough. Dogs with insufficient nutrition may be more competitive and defensive about resources, feeling their survival depends on acquiring and securing available food. In addition, the quality and ingredients of what they consume can have a tremendous influence on their affect and behavior. While dogs are, quintessentially, still the evolutionary master garbage disposal able to digest anything remotely edible, they have their limits. Some dogs have significant dietary intolerances and requirements, and food allergies to various proteins and other common ingredients in dog food. It is important to find the right diet for each dog, one that fits his distinct needs.

## ♥ Disability

**VULNERABILITY.** Disabled canines get along incredibly well, navigating their terrain and daily challenges with an admirable optimistic spirit. Most of the time, they are able to make the necessary adjustments to make do despite their clear disadvantage. Dogs know that they are more vulnerable when they are compromised in any way, and may easily feel threatened by conditions in their environment and by other individuals. Their ability to fight or flee in a precarious situation may be in jeopardy, and they know that they're unable to defend themselves or get away as quickly as other dogs. If your dog has a disability of any kind, be sensitive to the possibility that, beneath his resilient exterior, he may feel stressed, frightened, or even defensive.

## ♥ Individual:

**EVERYONE'S DIFFERENT.** Dogs have likes, dislikes, opinions, tastes, quirks, and preferences just as we do. Some of these individual traits may be influenced by your dog's prior experiences and learning, his environment, and even his genetics. But some of them just *are*, and may even fly in the face of other factors (like laid-back terriers that don't bark and herding dogs who have zero interest in chasing). It is important to observe your unique dog and ask yourself what motivates him as an individual to behave in certain ways, rather than making assumptions. Some dogs are highly motivated by treats, while others are way more into toys. Some dogs love praise and attention, and others prefer to keep their own space. And every dog will like some toys better than others, one food and not another, one person's touch and reject the next. Even these opinions and values can change. What motivated him yesterday could bore him today. What worked to keep his attention in one moment can fail the next time around in the face of something more interesting.

**DOGS HAVE BAD DAYS, TOO.** Owners often panic when their beloved, well-behaved, wonderful friend has "one of those days." The truth is, just like us, dogs will have days where their brain just isn't working great, when they are inexplicably tired or grumpy, when they can't seem to get anything right. If a bad day is an exception, and you don't observe a pattern of strange behavior over days or weeks, chances are it was just a blip on the screen. Sometimes all there is to do is conclude it was a crappy day and move on. Tomorrow will come around soon enough, and chances are you can both forget today ever happened.

When behaviors are not adding up or seem out of character, or sudden changes in your dog's demeanor or habits occur, consider the possibility that something in his internal world is amiss. If you suspect that this is the case, you should always, first and foremost, consult with your veterinarian, whose knowledge about many of the self-related symptoms may shed a great deal of light on a situation. That diagnosis of a urinary tract infection may make you finally understand why he has been struggling with his housetraining. The knowledge that he was an intact male for eight years makes his propensity for marking on all of your girlfriend's houseplants a little more understandable. Remembering his bad leg and the arthritis he suffers can calm your nerves a bit when he decides to lie down in the middle of the street on the walk home and go no further. Your first instinct may have been to assume he was just being a troublemaker, but now you realize that he is responding to those inner conditions of body and mind the way that any one of us would.

For all of the insights the other pillars of L.E.G.S.® can provide, your dog's self will ultimately only be his own. Gather up all of the details that you can about your dog's unique internal conditions and experiences. You can measure and test, diagnose and treat, recognize and resolve many of the health variables influencing his behavior. And you can enjoy his personal quirks, and the things life has taught him that influence his behavior. You can appreciate where he is in his personal development. Knowing as much as you can will allow you to have a thousand perfect moments with your bizarre and beautiful, green-ball-crazy, bed-stealing bozo. He is that one in a million. He is Bob.

No matter how much we wish that we could avoid having expectations about a relationship—no matter how much we dream of simply giving someone we love the room to be who they are—the truth is that we are going to have expectations anyway. Though wise men may council us in the art of mastering nonattachment (and there is much to be said for such an endeavor), most of us will find that expectations—about people, situations, experiences, and even our animal companions—are inevitable.

This is the most natural thing in the world. We are not the only species that attempts to anticipate the environmental circumstances we may encounter. Our genes are primed to expect certain events to occur in our lives, designed as we are to fit perfectly within a unique orchestra of conditions specific to our niche in the world. The experiences we have teach us how to live and survive; and, if we are learning well, we are constantly adding to our expectations about the world around us. We do this without even realizing it.

The problem we run into is that we often fabricate unrealistic expectations about life, especially about relationships and the behaviors of those around us. Without meaning to, we create impossible or arbitrary standards to which we feel others should conform. Unchecked expectations can lead to a host of misunderstandings, resentments, and false assumptions. We may miss out on the chance to know someone, to meet them at all, because we are so caught up in the fact that they have failed to live up to an ideal we have in our minds. When we are incorrect in our presumptions, we don't give them the break they need. We give up. All because we had incomplete information.

There is no reason for you to feel badly about having expectations of your dog. He will certainly have expectations of you—that you let him out to pee in the morning, that you feed him his breakfast every day, that you return from work at the end of the day. It's only reasonable that you have expectations of him, too.

Having a realistic understanding of what your dog needs will allow you to adjust your expectations about your dog. The big picture of your dog's L.E.G.S.® can help you to authentically prepare for the life you will share together. You can learn what you might expect from your dog's learning, environment, genetics, and self. You will both be better off if you have a clearer idea about what could be coming down the pike. It is really just about being honest, and finding the terms you can agree on, based on the needs and limitations you both have. Trust is what happens when, time and time again, you meet in the middle.

At the same time, for all the many benefits of expectations, do your best to remain flexible about them. Be willing to be wrong, and you may find yourself pleasantly surprised. Your dog could always be the exception, the one that breaks the mold. Nature does that from time to time.

There are no fixed rules, only guiding insights and information from which we can piece together a more logical and complete framework of ideas. The point here is to simply develop more *realistic* expectations of your canine friend. The last thing you want is to set him up for failure time and again because you are simply misinformed, unaware of what you have been missing.

The mysteries of our dogs' behaviors and our relationships with them are far from solved. But we have a *whole lot more* to go on than we did. Dedicated researchers, scientists, and professionals have provided us with more useful grist for the mill than we had in the past. You may as well be given the chance to take it all in and try to use it, for your dog's sake as well as your own.

This book isn't exhaustive. But it is, I hope, highly provocative—a catalyst for a paradigm shift in our current thinking about dogs. My hope is that it can be the ice-breaking, cage-shaking, appetite-whetting first step toward a new and more successful road for people and their canine companions—for you and your dog. L.E.G.S.® is simply the beginning, an introduction.

You already love your dog (or will soon if you are thinking about taking him home). Now I would like you to *meet your dog.* As best you can. Halfway. Equipped with the kind of sensible expectations and appropriate measures that may make life easier for both of you. Hopefully I can spare you some heartache with what I have learned from science, from practice, and from so many amazing dogs and their owners. Your relationship will always have its ups and downs, as any relationship will. But if I can open your eyes to your dog's perspective, even a little bit more, and in doing so bring you closer, then this book has made the difference I have dreamed for it to make.

So go ahead, drool over his adorable picture. Whether that face is already looking back at you in a frame on your nightstand or on that website just waiting to be found—your dog is ready to be met. You'll find each other very soon.

# SOURCES

1. Genetic Science Learning Center, "Epigenetics and Inheritance" (July, 2013). http://learn.genetics.utah.edu/content/epigenetics/inheritance/

2. Genetic Science Learning Center, "Epigenetics and Inheritance."

3. Liane Giemsch, Susanne C. Feine, Kurt W. Alt, Qiaomei Fu, Corina Knipper, Johannes Krause, Sarah Lacy, Olaf Nehlich, Constanze Niess, Svante Pääbo, Alfred Pawlik, Michael P. Richards, Verena Schünemann, Martin Street, Olaf Thalmann, Johann Tinnes, Erik Trinkaus, and Ralf W. Schmitz, "Interdisciplinary investigations of the late glacial double burial from Bonn-Oberkassel," Hugo Obermaier Society for Quaternary Research and Archaeology of the Stone Age: 57th Annual Meeting in Heidenheim (April 7-11, 2015).

4. Mietje Germonpré, "Fossil dogs and wolves from Palaeolithic sites in Belgium, the Ukraine and Russia: osteometry, ancient DNA and stable isotopes," *Journal of Archaeological Science* (February, 2009).

5. Raymond Coppinger and Lorna Coppinger, *Dogs: A New Understanding of Canine Origin, Behavior and Evolution* (University of Chicago Press, 2002).

6. Henri Lhote, *The Search for the Tassili Frescoes.* (E.P. Dutton, 1959).

7. Kathryn A. Bard, "The Egyptian Predynastic: A review of the Evidence," *Journal of Field Archaeology* (Autumn, 1994).

8. John Baines, "Symbolic Roles of Canine Figures on Early Monuments," *Archeo-Nil* (1993).

9. Coppinger and Coppinger, *Dogs.*

10. James E. Johannes, "Basenji Origin and Migration: Through the African Threshold," *The Official Bulletin of the Basenji Club of America* (July, August, September, 2005).

11. Edward of Norwich, *The Master of Game* (1413).

12. Ria Hörter, "Wolf Hunting with Dogs in Western and Central Europe," *The Canine Chronicle* (May, 2016),

13. Li Q, Liu Z, Li Y, et al., "Origin and phylogenetic analysis of Tibetan Mastiff based on the mitochondrial DNA sequence," *Journal of Genetics and Genomics* (June, 2008).

14. Liz Palika, *The Howell Book of Dogs: The Definitive Reference to 300 Breeds and Varieties* (John Wiley & Sons, 2007).

15. Brian Peckinpaugh, *Natural Born Guardians, History of the Dogs* (2016). http://naturalbornguardians.com/history-of-the-dogs/

16. Norwich, *The Master of Game.*

17. Coppinger and Coppinger, *Dogs.*

18. Elaine T. Ostrander, "Genetics and the Shape of Dogs: Studying the new sequence of the canine genome shows how tiny genetic changes can create enormous variation within a single species," *American Scientist* (Sept.–Oct. 2007).

19. Peter Savolainen, Ya-ping Zhang, Jing Luo, Joakim Lundeberg, and Thomas Leitner, "Genetic Evidence for an East Asian Origin of Domestic Dogs" *Science Magazine* (November 22, 2002).

20. David Hancock, *The Mastiffs: The Big Game Hunters—Their History, Development and Future* (Charwynne Dog Features, 2001).

21. American Kennel Club, "Scenthound History" (no date). http://www.akc.org/events/coonhound/history/

22. J. Busuttil, "The Maltese Dog," *Greece & Rome* (October, 1969).

23. Bud Boccone, "The Maltese, Toy Dog of Myth and Legend," American Kennel Club (2015). http://www.akc.org/content/entertainment/articles/maltese-toy-dog-myth-legend/

24. Clifford L.B. Hubbard, *Dogs in Britain, A Description of All Native Breeds and Most Foreign Breeds in Britain* (1948).

25. Jason J. Crean, "Zoo Genetics—Key Aspects of Conservation Biology," Chicago Zoological Society (2007).

26. American Kennel Club, "Scenthound History."

27. Fernand Mery, *The Life, History and Magic of the Dog* (Grosset & Dunlap, 1970).

28. Peter A. Levine, *Waking the Tiger: Healing Trauma—The Innate Capacity to Transform Overwhelming Experiences* (North Atlantic Books, 1997).

29. Giovanni Morsiani, *Short History of the Breed and Current Situation*, Lagotto Romagnolo Club of America (2017). http://www.lagottous.com/History

30. Morsiani, *Short History of the Breed.*

31. Carla Molinari, *The Portuguese Water Dog* (1988).

32. Jose Barba Coate "Razas Espanolas: El Perro De Aguas," *Todo Perro* (May, 1996).

33. Andre Dollinger, "Fishing, Hunting, Fowling" (2001). http://www.reshafim.org.il/ad/egypt/timelines/topics/fishing_and_hunting.htm

34. Norwich, *The Master of Game.*

35. Norwich, *The Master of Game.*

36. Morsiani, *Short History of the Breed.*

37. Molinari, *The Portuguese Water Dog.*

38. Coate, *Todo Perro.*

39. John Caius, *Of Englishe Dogges: The Diversities, the Names, the Natures, and the Properties* (1576).

40. Charles Fergus, *Gun Dog Breeds, A Guide to Spaniels, Retrievers, and Pointing Dogs* (Globe Pequot Press, 2002).

41. Gilbert Leighton-Boyce, *A Survey of Early Setters* (self-published, 1985).

42. Joseph Beete Jukes, *Excursions In and About Newfoundland During the Years 1839 and 1840* (John Murray, 1842).

43. Arliss Paddock, "The Retrievers: Ever Talented and Willing to Please," American Kennel Club (May, 2015). http://www.akc.org/content/entertainment/articles/the-retrievers-ever-talented-and-willing-to-please/

44. John Leslie, *The History of Scotland 1436–1561.*

45. Count Jacques du Fouilloux, *La Vernarie* (The Art of Hunting) (1560).

46. Patrick Burns, *American Working Terriers* (Lulu.com, 2006).

47. C. N. Trueman, "Dogs In World War One" (April, 2015). http://www.historylearningsite.co.uk/world-war-one/the-western-front-in-world-war-one/animals-in-world-war-one/dogs-in-world-war-one/

48. Unknown author, "The plague of rats in the French trenches," *The Illustrated War News* (February, 1916).

49. M. B. Wynn, *The History of the Mastiff* (Melton Mowbray, 1886).

50. Robert Leighton, *The New Book of the Dog* (Cassell, 1907).

51. Mike Homan, *A Complete History of Fighting Dogs* (Howell Book House, 1999).

52. Caius, *Of Englishe Dogges*.

53. Caius, *Of Englishe Dogges*.

54. Robert Jenkins and Ken Mollett, *The Story of the Real Bulldog* (TFH Publications, 1998).

55. Paul Richard, "A Steak in the Heart of Britain," *The Washington Post* (April 2, 1996).

56. Caius, *Of Englishe Dogge*.

57. Norwich, *The Master of Game*.

58. Rhonda D. Evans and Craig J. Forsyth, "Entertainment to Outrage: A Social Historical View of Dogfighting," *International Review of Modern Sociology*, Volume 27 (Autumn, 1997).

59. Various, "Bear Baiting and Bull Baiting," *Encyclopedia Britannica*, Volume 3 (1911).

60. Various, *The Illustrated London Reading Book* (1850).

61. Norwich, *The Master of Game*.

62. Various, *Illustrated London Reading Book*.

63. Marina Kuzina, "Brief History of the Samoyed," *Newsletter of the Primitive Aboriginal Dogs Society* (2004).

64. Vera Vasilyevena Volkova, "Forgotten Expedition," *Newsletter of the Primitive Aboriginal Dogs Society* (2006).

## DOGS IN THIS BOOK

*All photos taken by Jason Hewitt.*

### NATURAL DOG

Photo 1—Siberian Husky. Dog's name: Misfit. Owner's name: Casey Towne

Photo 2—Basenji. Dog's name: C-Quest Jokuba No Matter What "Geddy". Owner's name: Russella Bowen

Photo 3—Akita. Dog's name: Willow. Owner's name: Patti and Stand Claridge

Photo 4—Shiba Inu. Dog's name: Scout. Owner's name: Katelyn Phillips

### SIGHT HOUND

Photo 1—Ibizan Hound. Dog's name: Fin. Owner's name: Robin Davis

Photo 2—Borzoi. Dog's name: GCH Lagniappe Cajun "Zydeco" Bon-Ton. Owner's name: Cindy Michalak

Photo 3—Whippet. Dog's name: Devereux Simply Deco "Conner." Owner's name: Rachel Gongre

### GUARDIAN

Photo 1—Great Pyrenees. Dog's name: Bane. Owner's name: Leah Ball

Photo 2—St. Bernard. Dog's name: Le Phaire's Brutus Maximus. Owner's name: Leanna Forehand

Photo 3—Boerboel. Dog's name: Bella. Owner's name: anonymous

Photo 4—Greater Swiss Mountain Dog. Dog's name: Maggie. Owner's name: Linda Cunningham

## TOY DOG

Photo 1—Maltese. Dog's name: Zelda. Owner's name: Barbara Lenschmidt

Photo 2—Tibetan Spaniel/Chihuahua mix. Dog's name: Nugget. Owner's name: Jamie Roper

Photo 3—Phalene Papillon. Dog's name: Tia. Owner's name: Sharon Mitchell

Photo 4—Pug. Dog's name: Gertrude. Owner's name: Ashley Branham

## SCENT HOUND

Photo 1—Bloodhound. Dog's name: Gracie. Owner's name: James and Jocelyn Tate

Photo 2—Bassett Hound. Dog's name: Ben. Owner's name: Ginna Reid

Photo 3—Treeing Walker Coonhound. Dog's name: Lucy. Owner's name: Lynne Brofman

Photo 4—Treeing Walker Coon Hound. Dog's name: Beatrix. Owner's name: Andrea Roberts

## GUN DOG

Photo 1— Golden Retriever. Dog's name: Whopper. Owner's name: Molly Norton

Photo 2—German Shorthair Pointer. Dog's name: Gunner. Owner's name: Joseph Davenport

Photo 3—Vizsla. Dog's name: Riddley. Owner's name: Billy Robinson

Photo 4—English Springer Spaniel. Photo taken by: Jason Hewitt. Dog's name: Starla. Owner's name: Adam J. Smith

## TERRIER

Photo 1—Norwich Terrier. Dog's name: Reba. Owner's name: Norma Braun

Photo 2—Wire Fox Terrier. Dog's name: Tracy. Owner's name: Thomas Roth

Photo 3— Jack Russell Terrier. Dog's name: Emmitt. Owner's name: Lisa Yoli

Photo 4—Border Terrier. Dog's name: Birdie. Owner's name: Danielle Arceneaux

## BULL DOG

Photo 1—American Staffordshire Terrier. Dog's name: Hagan. Owner's name: Mark and Adriana Darwish

Photo 2—Bull Terrier. Dog's name: Fiona. Owner's name: Ilana Mcallister

Photo 3—American Pit Bull Terrier. Dog's name: Bahama. Owner's name: Bill and Tanya Higgins

Photo 4—English Bull Dog. Dog's name: Miyagi. Owner's name: Jessica Stone

## HERDING DOG

Photo 1—Australian Cattle Dog. Dog's name: Riley. Owner's name: Lew Springer

Photo 2—Australian Shepherd. Dog's name: Atasi. Owner's name: Tracey Norrell

Photo 3—Shetland Sheepdog/Pembroke Welsh Corgi mix. Dog's name: Sammy. Owner's name: Mary Donnelly

Photo 4—Border Collie. Dog's name: Juno. Owner's name: Patti and Stan Claridge

## WORLD DOG

Photo 1—tan and white mix. Dog's name: Sally. Owner's name: Tarah and Dave Plavac

Photo 2—red mix. Dog's name: Tyler. Owner's name: Carrie Uehlein

Photo 3—black mix. Dog's name: Salvador. Owner's name: Josslyn Gray

Photo 4—black and white mix. Dog's name: Luna. Owner's name: Allegra Grant

## ACKNOWLEDGMENTS

I would like to express my deep and heartfelt gratitude to the many individuals who have contributed to the final manifestation of this project. I could not have done it without each and every one of you.

To my parents, Paul and Bonnie, who have supported my obsession with dogs since I was two years old, fostering my passion with an unwavering commitment to helping me to follow my dreams. You are my rocks.

To my children, Sam and Sally, who have been far more patient, understanding, and generous about the demands that this book presented to their mom's time than any kid should have to be. You are my beacons.

To my husband, Jason Hewitt, for being the love of my life twenty years ago, for keeping the box, the ring, and key to my heart all that time, and for giving me a second chance so many years later as we created this book together. You are my peace.

To my manager, Emily Miller, for being the most valuable and enthusiastic right hand a business owner could ever ask for, and an exceptional and hilarious friend I am fortunate enough to work with every day. You are my irreplaceable porcelain.

To my clients, who have opened their lives, stories, and hearts to me for seventeen years and shared with me your honest challenges, questions, hopes, successes, failures, and love for your dogs. You are my inspiration.

To the dogs who have opened my eyes to the truth of their experiences, trusted me, and allowed me to work with them as a mediator and friend. You are my teachers.

To my colleagues and friends who have spent moments or hours with me in conversation exchanging ideas with curiosity and excitement, determined to ask the hardest questions and tackle difficult goals for the betterment of animals and people. You are my community.

To Don Livingston, for believing in me and the vision of LEGS, and making it all possible with your tremendous generosity. You were the fuel.

To Ray Coppinger, for being honest about dogs, for believing in my efforts to bring the sciences together for dog owners, for writing the foreword to this book, and for your good humor and friendship. You were the match.

To the scientists and researchers, for all of your incredible dedication, hard work, and discoveries upon which this project has been built. You were my ingredients.

To Kris Dahl and ICM, for taking a chance on a first-time author and embracing the vision of this book. You were the door.

To Pippa White and Chronicle Books, for recognizing the importance of this project and for the creativity and insights you have brought the process. You were the vehicle.

To the many animal companions I have had the honor to share my life with over the years, for showing me the things no person could show me, for sharing love with me no person could give, for taking me to all of those wild places, and leading me forward towards the next questions and answers. You are the simple miracles behind it all.

## ABOUT THE AUTHOR

Kim Brophey is an applied ethologist, certified dog behavior consultant, and developer of the L.E.G.S.® dog behavior model and Dog Key™ software. She considers herself a lifetime dog nerd. Kim lives in Asheville, North Carolina, where she operates The Dog Door, a modern dog behavior center and storefront, as well as Dog City, USA, a resource center for local and visiting dogs and their humans. Kim shares her mountain home with one impossibly patient husband, two remarkably inspiring kids, and a host of other ridiculous dogs and cats.